ARAB AIR FORCES

By Charles Stafrace
Color by Don Greer & Tom Tullis

squadron/signal publications

A pair of Egyptian Air Force MiG-15bis fighters fly formation with Hawker Hunters of the Iraqi Air Force and Royal Jordanian Air Force over the Sinai desert in the early 1960s.

If you have any photographs of aircraft, armor, soldiers or ships of any nation, particularly wartime snapshots, why not share them with us and help make Squadron/Signal's books all the more interesting and complete in the future. Any photograph sent to us will be copied and the original returned. The donor will be fully credited for any photos used. Please send them to:

Squadron/Signal Publications, Inc.
1115 Crowley Drive
Carrollton, TX 75011-50101

Acknowledgments

The photographs used in this work have been collected over the last quarter century and, unfortunately, I cannot remember with accuracy the origin of a small number of them. All others have been duly credited to the contributor. For those who remain uncredited, I hope I will be forgiven. To all contributors, I extend my most grateful thanks, for without their cooperation this book could not have been completed.

Forward

The events of the past years in the Middle East have been only the latest in a series of conflicts which many believe to have started in 1949. Indeed, the history of the area in the past half century has been dominated by five main factors: the creation of the State of Israel, shifting alliances between Arab states and Western and Eastern Blocs, rivalries among the states (some of ancient origins), the disunity of the Arab World despite various attempts to promote unity and the West's dependence on Arab oil.

The first and last of these factors have brought the Arab countries more or less together, but the other elements have been the cause of a great deal of strife, disorder, coups, border clashes and even outright war among/between the Arab states. In these events, combat aircraft have been recognized by all as an essential weapon and the development of Arab air power has, therefore, been a dramatic one.

It is a little realized fact that in the early 1930s two Arab Air Forces, those of Egypt and Iraq, had already been established. It is even less recognized that the very first use of the aircraft as an aerial weapon took place over an Arab country — Libya. This occurred when an Italian Air Force Taube aircraft "bombed" enemy positions on 1 November 1911, during the Italian Turkish War. Since that time aviation has progressed within the Arab world, particularly since the 1970s, when the soaring price of petroleum, of which Arab countries control a major portion of the world's reserves, made it possible for some air forces within the region to obtain the best and latest in combat aircraft.

In the following account I have tried to narrate, in brief the history of each of the air forces that make up the Arab world.

Overleaf: An F-4E Phantom II of the N0 222 Tactical Fighter Brigade, Egyptian Air Force flies over the Pyramids during the early 1980s. A total of thirty-four F-4s were delivered to Egypt. (McDonnell-Douglas)

Algeria
Al Quwwat al Jawwiya al Jaza'erlya (Algerian Air Force)

Algeria won independence from France on 3 July 1962 after a long and violent struggle for freedom which had started in 1954. At the peak of the Algerian war, France had deployed no less than 800 aircraft and a million troops to the colony.

On independence, Algeria established an air arm with the assistance of Egypt which donated eighteen Gomhouria primary trainers. Owing to President Ben Bella's socialist tendencies, the Soviet Bloc agreed to Algeria's requests and East European technicians arrived in November of 1962 to set up an embryo air force consisting of five MiG-15UTI jet trainers, six Il-14 transports and ten Mi-4 helicopters donated by the USSR. Two Beech D 18S light transports were purchased for the personal use of President Ben Bella.

During 1963, a brief border war with Morocco, over an iron ore-rich territory, reminded Algeria of its vulnerability. The following year a program for the procurement of more military hardware and the re-activation of ex-French airfields was started.. Aircraft supplied from the Soviet Union during 1964/65 included four Il-18 transports, eight Il-14s, seven An-12 transports, twenty MiG-15bis fighters, thirty MiG-17F fighters, twelve Il-28 bombers and three Mi-1 helicopters. Training of Algerian air crews was undertaken in Egypt and China, while Egyptian instructors trained Algerian crews on the newly activated air bases.

In 1965, a military coup resulted in the replacement of Ben Bella's regime by a more moderate government. Over time, the former ties with the USSR were renewed. The Soviets, eager to balance the strong U.S. presence at Wheelus Air Base in Libya, agreed to the new Algerian government's requests for additional military aircraft. During 1966 the Soviets delivered more MiG-17Fs and Il-28s, along with the first six of thirty-seven MiG-21F Fishbed C fighters and twenty Mi-4 helicopters, half of which were equipped with armament for the ground attack role. Most aircraft within the Algerian Air Force were, however, still being flown by foreign pilots, due to a shortage of trained Algerian personnel.

During the Arab-Israeli Six Day War of June 1967, Algerian Air Force (AAF) fighter and bomber units (Il-28s and MiG-21s) were hurried to Egypt, but only the MiGs reached the battle zone in time. Six of the fighters were reported to have been captured by the IDF/AF when they landed at El Arish airfield, which had just been lost to the Israelis.

Although five new SA-330 Puma helicopters and twenty-eight ex-West German Fouga Magister jet trainers were purchased from France in 1969, Algeria's main source of aircraft procurement remained the Soviet Union. By 1970, the AAF could muster over 200 aircraft and

Many North African countries allocate civil-like registrations to their military transports and, occasionally, trainers. This Antonov An-12 Cub A of the Algerian Air Force carries such a registration (7T-WAC) on the fuselage along with a military serial (514). The aircraft carries a fin flash but no roundels. (J. Visanich)

helicopters, comprising an air defense regiment of three squadrons with thirty-five MiG-21F interceptors, a ground attack regiment with forty MiG-17Fs (these having a secondary interception role), a light bomber squadron with Il-28s, an operational conversion unit with MiG-15 fighters and trainers and two transport squadrons flying eight An-12s, fourteen Il-14s and three Il-18s. Training was conducted with 18 Gomhourias, twelve Avia C.11 and the Fouga Magisters, while the old Beech D 18S were still flying VIP duties. Helicopters included forty Mi-4s, three Mi-1 and seven Hughes 269As, the latter two types being retained for training purposes.

In 1971 an eighteen year agreement was signed with the USSR permitting the basing of Soviet forces on Algerian bases. As a result, a force of V-VS MiG-25 Foxbat and Su-7 Fitters deployed to Algeria (the aircraft were painted in Algerian markings as a political necessity . Twenty Su-7s were also delivered to the AAF during 1973, supplementing the MiG-17Fs in the ground attack role. A squadron of Su-7s were sent to Egypt during the 1973 Yom Kipper War, but there is no evidence that they actually saw action.

During this period Algeria made a number of small western purchases including: six Fokker F-27 Friendship transports, a Beech King Air, three Beech Super King Airs, three Beech Queen Airs and two Canadair CL-215 amphibians for fire-fighting duties.

By 1978, the MiG-21 fleet had been reinforced by the arrival of upgraded MiG-21MF and MiG-21bis Fishbed J/L/N variants, about ninety of which were in service. In addition some forty MiG-23BM, 23MF and 23U Floggers were delivered and during the next year a number of MiG-25 and MiG-25R Foxbats along with some twenty-four Su-20 swing-wing fighters. These late model Fitters supplemented the earlier Su-7s in the ground attack role.

Recognizing the need for a good training infrastructure, six Beech T-34C Turbo-Mentors and 3 Beech 200 trainers were purchased during 1978/79, replacing the old Avia C.11 and Gomhourias. Algeria's mediation efforts helped gain the release of American hostages held in the Teheran Embassy during 1981 and the country was rewarded by a donation from the United States of six C-130H Hercules transports, to which

Other Algerian Air Force An-12 Cubs, like 7T-WAA also carried roundels on the fuselage and wings. The legend, Algerian Air Force appears on the starboard front fuselage while its Arabic equivalent is painted on the port side. (J.Visanich)

During 1981 the U.S. donated six C-130H Hercules transports to the Algerian Air Force, including 7T-WHY. It was finished in Green, Dark Green and Tan uppersurfaces with Light Blue undersurfaces and carries its registration in Black on the fin, starboard upper and port lower wing surfaces. (Lockheed)

Predominantly equipped with Soviet aircraft, Algeria made occasional purchases from the West including six Beech T-34C-1 Turbo-Mentors during 1978-79. Configured without underwing hardpoints and delivered in both civil and military registrations, they were absorbed in the inventory of the National Pilots School at Oran, an ostensibly civil flying establishment which also trains students in instrumental and aerobatic flying for the military. (G.J.Kamp)

Later in their service careers, Algerian T-34Cs were given a Dark Brown/Sand camouflage finish with the national insignia carried in six positions. (Beechcraft)

Algeria later added a further twelve, seven of which were C-130H-30s. The arrival of these transports enabled the AAF to retire the An-12s from front-line service.

During the early 1990s, the AAF's main strike force consisted of some sixty MiG-23s in various versions, as well as over thirty Su-20s, although the MiG-21, of which some eighty are believed to be still in service, was numerically the most important type.

Over thirty MiG-25 Foxbats form an interceptor-reconnaissance unit and two-seat versions of this type may indicate that advanced training is now being undertaken locally. In 1988, Algeria had shown interest in obtaining the MiG-29 Fulcrum, but Russia now is more interested in furnishing military hardware on a commercial basis, rather than for strategic motives, putting the MiG-29s out of reach for the Algerian Air Force. One of the latest acquisitions was twenty-four Aero L-39ZA Albatros armed trainers which were delivered between 1987-1990 as replacements for the Fouga Magisters.

Bahrain
Bahrain Amiri Air Force

When the United Arab Emirates was formed during 1971 by the amalgamation of the sheikdoms that made up the ex-British Trucial States, Bahrain declined to join and preferred to remain independent. Before that time, Muharraq Island, which belonged to Bahrain, was an important staging post for RAF aircraft. Britain's withdrawal from the Middle and Far East during the late 1960s/early 1970s considerably reduced Bahrain's importance. Oil was, and still is, Bahrain's main economic asset.

The first military aircraft purchased by the country was a Westland Scout Mk.1 Srs.4 helicopter which was received by the Bahrain State Police during 1965. This was followed by a second aircraft a year later. In 1977 the Bahrain Amiri Air Force (BAAF) was established with two MBB Bo-105C helicopters, a third one being added the following year. The State Police continued to operate independently, while a third force, the Bahrain Public Security established an air arm during 1979 by the acquisition of a Bell 205A which was subsequently joined by a Hughes 269C, two other Hughes 269s going to the State Police. These three independent forces operated under the overall responsibility of the Bahrain Defense Force.

Rotary-winged craft for liaison and communications remained the sole equipment of the Amiri Air Force and the other governmental agencies. The BAAF acquired two Hughes 369Ds during 1979. These were used for training and observation sorties from Bahrain International Airport, while an Agusta-Bell AB-212 was added to the inventory that same year. For its part, Public Security purchased two Bell 412 fifteen-seat helicopters; indeed this corps became the foremost of the three air branches of the Defense Force when it added two Sikorsky S-76A Spirits to the force during 1982.

Conflict in the Gulf caused by the Iran-Iraq War exposed Bahrain's weakness, especially in air defense, and for this reason the U.S. Defense

Department approved the sale of eight Northrop F-5E and four two-seat F-5F Tiger IIs to the BAAF, deliveries of which started in December of 1985. Full operational status on the Sidewinder-equipped F-5E/Fs had not yet been achieved when Bahrain, during 1987, supported by the Gulf Cooperation Council (Saudi Arabia, United Arab Emirates, Kuwait, Qatar, Oman and Bahrain), concluded a 400 million dollar arms package with General Dynamics for the supply of eight F-16C and four F-16D two-seat Fighting Falcons, the first examples of which were received in March of 1990.

Construction of a new air base, Sheik Isa, at Sitrah, south of Manama on the main island of Bahrain, was completed to receive the F-16s, the other two main airfields being Manama Airport and the ex-RAF base at Muharraq. In 1992, the BAAF received eight McDonnell-Douglas AH-64 Apache anti-armor helicopters, along with some four hundred Hellfire anti-tank guided missiles.

A number of aircraft are operated in the VIP transport role, including a Grumman Gulfstream II used by the Amir (head of state). This aircraft operates from the civil airport at Manama (the capital and main administrative center in Bahrain).

The BAAF is a small, compact force capable of defending the small national territory although dependence on foreign aircrews remains quite high, which could cause problems in the event of a conflict.

The Bahrain Amiri Air Force (BAAF) equipment had consisted of rotary winged aircraft unitl the arrival of eight Northrop F-5E and four F-5F Tiger IIs during 1982. These aircraft were initially based at Manama on Muharraq Island, they were moved to Sheik Isa Air Base when the facility was completed during 1989. (Northrop)

Bahrain was the first Persian Gulf country to operate the General Dynamics/Lockheed F-16 when the first of twelve F-16C/Ds entered service during March of 1990. The unit is based at Sheik Isa Air Base, which was built especially to house the Fighting Falcons. Most of the arms package was financed with funds from the Gulf Cooperation Council. (GD)

Egypt

Al Quwwat al Jawwiya al Misriya (Egyptian Air Force)

Britain's connection with Egypt began during 1841, and greatly expanded after the opening of the Suez Canal in 1869. After the First World War, Britain proclaimed a protectorate over Egypt. Finally, in 1922, the British conceded independence to the kingdom. Becoming a monarchy when granted independence, Egypt re-organized its army and in 1930 laid plans for the establishment of an air arm. Under British guidance the Egyptian Army Air Force (EAAF) was born during November of 1931 at Almaza, near Cairo. In May of 1932 three Egyptian pilots, trained by the resident Royal Air Force unit at Abu Sueir, together with two British pilots flew five DH.60T Moths from Britain to Almaza. Another Moth and two Avro 618 Tens (Fokker F-VII-3m) were added that same year.

In 1933, the EAAF purchased ten Avro 626s, these and the Moths, equipped with cameras and bomb racks, being used for patrols over the

Ten Avro 626 Prefects were purchased by the fledgling Egyptian Army Air Force in November of 1933. Later, fifteen additional Avro 626s were purchased for a total of twenty-seven aircraft. The Avros saw service in the both the training and border patrol roles. (via Author)

The Hawker Audax version purchased by Egypt was powered by a radial Armstrong-Siddeley Panther, six aircraft being delivered in March 1937 and another eighteen in March/May 1938. This army cooperation biplane was also known as Avro 674 since it was also built by Avro. (via Author)

Sinai and Western Desert. In August of 1936 an Anglo-Egyptian Treaty gave Britain the right to station 10,000 men in the Canal Zone for twenty years, while responsibility of the EAAF fell fully on the Egyptians.

The response to aviation encouraged the EAAF to open a Flying Training School at Almaza and increase its fleet by fifteen additional Avro 626s, twenty-four Hawker Audaxs and three surplus ex-RAF Fairey Gordon Is. When the Second World War broke out the EAAF was re-organized as an autonomous force, becoming known as the Royal Egyptian Air Force (REAF). Nineteen Miles Magister trainers, eighteen Westland Lysander army-cooperation aircraft, three Avro Anson I transports and eighteen Gloster Gladiator I biplane fighters were purchased from Britain and by the end of 1939, the REAF was comprised of the following: No 1 (Army Cooperation) Squadron -Audax/Lysanders, No. 2 (Fighter) Squadron - Gladiators, No 3 (Communications) Squadron - Ansons/Avro 626s, No 4 (General Purpose) Squadron - Audax, Target Tow Flight - Gordon I, Royal Flight - Anson and the Flight Training School - Magister/DH.60T.

Airfields in use included Cairo, Almaza, Hellopolis, Qasaba, Mersa Matruh, Fuka, Amrlya (Alexandria), Maaten Baqqush, Sidi el-Barrani, Abu Sueir, Abouklr, Helwan, Sidi Haneish and Dekhe11a, these excluding those in the Canal Zone which were normally used and controlled the RAF. When Italy entered the war on Germany's side in June of 1940 Egypt preferred to declare neutrality. The RAF took over most of the available airfields leaving only Almaza for the REAF. The force operated from here to defend Cairo. By late 1942, twenty Hurricanes and a number of P-40C Tomahawks, all ex-RAF, entered REAF service, while in 1943 the first of several North American Harvards were absorbed into the Almaza FTS, followed later on in the war by twenty-six ex-RAF Miles Master trainers.

With the surrender of Axis forces in North Africa a number of ex-RAF Spitfire VBs/VCs were passed to the REAF, enabling the Gladiator fighter unit to be re-equipped, while some Anson Is were procured for anti-submarine patrols in the Red Sea. Five C-47s abandoned by the USAAF at Cairo were repaired and taken into service with the REAF. These were soon joined by another two, a11 seven being used to equip

This Hawker Audax (K401) flying over the Egyptian coast was one of the first batch received by the EAF. Aircraft of the second batch carried serial numbers in the K500 series. (S. Sharmy)

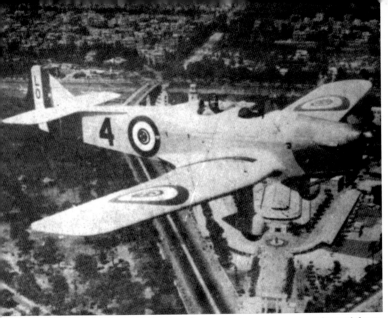

Eighteen Miles Magister primary trainers were purchased from Britain during 1938. Additional batches brought the total number of Magisters in REAF service to some forty-two aircraft. The Magister was operated by the Flying Training School of Almaza. (S. Sharmy) No 7 Squadron.

The end of the war in Europe rendered surplus hundreds of aircraft and twenty ex-RAF Spitfire IXcs and a number of Airspeed Oxford and DH Doves were delivered to the REAF, specialized training of Egyptian personnel now being offered by the British at training establishments in the U.K.

War with Israel 1948/49

In the post-war period, Arab anti-British feeling was inevitable when Britain did not stick to its Balfour Declaration of 1917, which called for an autonomous Arab state to be established in Palestine. The United Nations ruled that two new states should be created in Palestine, one Arab and one Jewish. While this was good enough for the Jews, the U.N. decision was not agreed to by the Arab states and on 15 May 1948, the day of Israel's creation, Egypt attacked the new state with Syria, Lebanon, Iraq and Jordan following suit.

An Israeli Air Force as such did not yet exist; however, during 1947 a clandestine force had been formed with a number of Piper Cubs, Auster AOPs and other similar British, U.S., Czech and Polish types, many being fitted with makeshift bomb racks. Israeli pilots were volunteers from Britain, the U.S., Canada, South Africa and other nations, mostly Second World War combat veterans. While the opposing Arab air forces collectively possessed superiority in both aircraft quality and quantity, the Israeli Air Force had a clear advantage in being manned by experi-

The Lysanders remained in service with the REAF until they were withdrawn during the Arab-Israeli war of 1948/49. It was found that their small bomb loads made them ineffective against strongly-fortified Israeli positions and their slow speed rendered them vulnerable to Israeli fighters. (Via G.J. Kamp)

The first of eighteen new production Westland Lysander I army cooperation aircraft for the REAF was received during 1939. These were followed by ex-RAF machines later, equipping No 1 Squadron which also flew one Atlas and some Hawker Audaxes. Y503 was the third machine delivered to the REAF. (S. Sharmy)

enced and battle-proven pilots, a fact which was to prove decisive in the war.

The Arab armies invaded Israel on three fronts, the REAF deploying a force of fifteen Spitfire LF.IXCs of No 2 Squadron to El Arish in the Sinai; five C-47s were modified to roll bombs from the side cargo doors, while a flight of Lysanders, which had re-equipped No 3 Squadron, were expected to fulfill their designated role of army cooperation. The REAF also "obtained" the services of the Hawker Fury prototype (NX798/G-AKRY) which was in Egypt while making a sales tour of the Middle East. The aircraft was commandeered, fitted with machine-guns from a Spitfire V and pressed into service. This aircraft in fact scored the first kill of the war when it shot down an Israeli Auster J-1 on 7 June.

On the first day of war, REAF Spitfires attacked Sde Dor airfield and Tel Aviv, damaging several aircraft on the ground with the loss of one Spitfire to anti-aircraft fire. The Lysanders supported the advance of Egyptian troops but their light bombs were ineffective against heavily fortified Israeli positions. The C-47 "bombers" raided Tel Aviv fuel dumps and transport depots, but their bombing was inaccurate. Spitfires

Apart from local conversions, particularly in the Soviet Union and South Africa, only twenty-one two-seat Spitfire T.9s were produced, one of which was exported to the REAF during 1950. Registered G-ALJM in Britain, it became 684 in REAF service. (via Author)

After having operated Merlin-engined Spitfire Vs and IXs in the war against Israel in 1948/49, the REAF placed an order for twenty reconditioned Griffon-engined Spitfire F. 22s in 1950. The advent of the jet fighter made even this late Spitfire variant obsolete before it entered service. (Via G.J. Kamp)

The Hawker Sea Fury epitomized the peak of British piston-engined fighter design; however, the accelerated development of jet fighters soon rendered the propeller-driven fighter obsolete. The REAF had purchased twelve new production land-based Fury Is during 1950 to replace the Spitfire Vs. The availability of such early jets as the Gloster Meteor F.4 and Vampire FB.5 led the REAF to assign the Furys to the ground attack mission. (Via G.J. Kamp)

were able to dislodge Israelis from their positions in Nitzanin and Isdad was captured on 7 June.

In the north, Syrian and Lebanese ground forces advanced into Israel, supported by Syrian Air Force armed Harvard trainers. The Israelis were more successful here and repulsed the attacks and even retook lost territory by 23 May. On the eastern front the Iraqi army, assisted by RIrAF Harvards, forded the Jordan River and advanced deep into Israel in a bid to cut the country in half. Recognizing this danger the Israelis mounted a counter attack, which arrested the Iraqi advance.

Israel negotiated the purchase of a number of Avia S-199 Mezecs (Bf 109s), forty ex-Czech Air Force Spitfire LF IXc and LF XVI and three P-51D Mustangs which were no longer required by the Czechs. During May the REAF contracted for forty-two Macchi C.205 Veltro fighters (eleven C.205s and thirty-one converted from C.202s), but only fifteen had been delivered to El Arish by the end of the war in January of 1949. The Italians also furnished seventeen Fiat G.55A Centauto fighters and two, two-seat G.55B trainers, none reaching operational status by the time the war ended.

The first operational use of Israel's S-199s was on 29 May when four aircraft attacked an Egyptian Army column advancing on Tel Aviv. One was shot down, another crashed at Herzlia and a third was lost the next day. On 3 June, an S-199 shot down a REAF C-47 "bomber" near Tel Aviv and damaged a second but a fourth S-199 was lost to ground fire from Iraqi troops near Nathanya. After the appearance of the S-199 the REAF ceased using its slow C-47s and Lysanders, and quickly deployed No 6 Squadron's Spitfire VCs to El Arish.

A truce imposed by the U.N. on 11 June enabled Israel to replenish its exhausted fleet of aircraft by procuring ten Bristol Beaufighters. On 9 July Israel broke the truce when a force of S-199s bombed Lydda and Ramleh with the loss of two aircraft but the attack enabled stalled Israeli armor to advance. On 17 July, three S199s pounced two REAF Spitfire

VCs which were engaged a ground attack mission near Al Majdal with the loss of one aircraft on each side. The first real heavy bombing raid of the war was made on 15 July when three Boeing B-17 Flying Fortresses attacked Cairo on their delivery flight from the U.S. to Israel. On the ground, the Israelis were slowly gaining the upper hand. Supported by armed Harvards with a top cover of S-199s and Spitfires, the Israeli army dislodged the Arabs from Lydda, widened a corridor to Jerusalem and opened a new corridor in the south to the Negev. A second truce on 18 July again gave both air forces breathing space to obtain more aircraft. The REAF purchased twelve Short Stirling freighters and retrofitted them to carry bombs. Lack of air crews trained on four engined aircraft, however, limited their use. 150 experienced volunteer pilots became available to the Israelis and when the truce expired on 15 October, the REAF found that its previous air supremacy had been lost to the Israelis. By 31 October all Galilee was retaken with the Egyptian forces retreating south to avoid encirclement. By that time, only Syrian Harvards were left to harass Israeli troops in the north. Israeli Air Force raids on El Arish, mostly by B-17s and Beaufighters, accompanied a rapid Israeli army advance. El Arish was in danger of being overrun and REAF Stirling bombers and the first of the Macchi C.205 Veltro fighters made desperate attacks to halt the Israelis, but on 30 December the Egyptians lost the airfield.

At this point Britain threatened to intervene and on 4 January asked Israel to withdraw from Egyptian territory, which Israel did. A cease fire was agreed upon two days later, but in the few days between the cease fire and the actual armistice air activity was quite intense. REAF aircraft claimed a Piper Cub, a Spitfire and two Harvards while five others were claimed destroyed by anti-aircraft fire. For its part, the Israeli Air Force claimed six Spitfires, eight Macchi C.205s and a C-47, these claims being denied by the REAF which, in fact, had lost only seven aircraft during that period.

By the end of the war, Israel had not only defended the land allocated to it by the U.N. but had added the coastal strip north of Gaza, the hinterland of Acre and a wide corridor to Jerusalem.

Re-equipment

A major rearmament program for the REAF was launched after the war. Nine Lancaster B.1 bombers and nine Halifax A.9 transports were purchased in 1950 but the availability problem of multi-engined aircraft crews remained and these types, particularly the Lancasters, remained at Almaza largely unused. Spitfire losses during the war were made good

The General Aero Organization of Heliopolis, Egypt built the Bu-181 under license under the name Gomhouria. Some 500 were built, in several versions, with most of the earlier marks going to the Air Academy at Bilbeis. These overall Yellow Mk 6s are believed to have been operated by a government-sponsored flying club. Later variants had a new single-piece canopy and clear-vision windscreen. Around a hundred Mk.6s and Mk.8Rs remain in service today with the Egyptian AF. (S. Sharmy)

A Heliopolis-built Gomhouria trainer of the EAF during the early 1950s. This aircraft was one of the first off the Egyptian production line. It appears to be overall Natural Metal finish with the Green/White/Green national insignia, although no serial number is visible. (EAF)

The EAF received twelve Gloster Meteor F.4 and three Meteor T-7s during 1949. The Meteors were the first jet fighters to see service in the EAF and were followed by other Meteor variants including the F.8 and NF.13. (via Glenn Ashley)

by the purchase of twenty Spitfire F.22s during 1950/51, these being accompanied by a single Spitfire T.9 trainer. Twelve Hawker Fury Is, brought up to Sea Fury FB 11 standards, were also contracted for during 1950, these being used to replace the fighter-bomber Spitfires in the REAF. But even prior to the delivery of these piston engined types, the Egyptians had made efforts to purchase twelve DH Vampire night fighters along with a number of Gloster Meteor F.4s and T.7s, but were foiled by an arms embargo imposed by Britain on all combatants of the 1948/49 war. In October of 1949, during a temporary lifting of the ban, an order for twelve Meteor F.4s and three Meteor T.7s was filled. In addition, the Egyptians struck a deal with the Italians, who built the Vampire FB.52 under license, and thirty fighters were delivered. With the final lifting of the embargo the REAF ordered a further forty-nine Vampire FB.52s from Britain in August of 1953 and twelve Vampire T.55s in early 1955, all aircraft being delivered over the next few years. Twelve ex-RAF Meteor F.8s were ordered, the final five of which were received during 1955 accompanied by six Meteor NF.13 night fighters.

The FTS at Almaza was bolstered by the creation of an Air Academy at Bilbeis during 1950 where all remaining Harvards and Miles Masters were transferred for basic training. That year Egypt obtained a license from Czechoslovakia to manufacture the German Bucker Bu-181D

The standard Soviet light jet bomber of the 1950s was the Il-28 Beagle. Most Soviet client states received the type, the Egyptian Air Force taking delivery of thirty-nine aircraft during 1955. Initially based at Cairo West, a number of the Il-28s were wiped out by Anglo-French air strikes during the 1956 Suez campaign. Twenty-eight were quickly evacuated south to Luxor, thought to be out of range of the British/French aircraft, but on 4 November 1956 French F-84Fs reached Luxor and destroyed twenty of the Beagles. (S. Sharmy)

The MiG-15bis Fagot was the first Soviet fighter to enter Egyptian service. This MiG-15bis, serial 2702, carries the Red/White/Black roundel with two Green stars adopted after the creation of the Union of Arab Republics with Syria and Yemen in 1958. The Black bands around the rear fuselage and wing tips were a common feature of EAF fighters of the time (although some aircraft carried Green/White bands). The insignia on the nose is unidentified. (S. Sharmy)

Bestmann. Locally named the Gomhouria, the trainer was soon coming off the Heliopolis production line and hundreds were to be produced.

British presence was then being seen as an affront to Egyptian nationhood and the 1936 agreement, which still had 5 years to run, was abrogated by Egypt during October of 1951. Anti-British riots in Cairo caused a confused situation which was taken advantage of by a group of Free Officers who deposed the King in January of 1952 and proclaimed a republic in June of 1953, causing the "royal" title to be removed from all national organizations, including the air force. Two years after the revolution Colonel Nasser was named President of Egypt, but relations with Britain were not bad, although arms supplies were being made on a piece-meal basis. Agreement on the evacuation of the Canal Zone was reached in July of 1954 and by March of 1956, all RAF bases were handed over to the Egyptian Air Force (EAF).

In the meantime Israel had befriended France and had purchased Ouragan and Mystere IV fighters and Noratlas transports, while Britain also provided the Israelis with Meteor F.8s and FR 9s. An alarmed Egypt started to look elsewhere for an uninterrupted supply of arms and in September of 1955 an Egyptian-Czech deal was concluded which

MiG-15UTI Midget trainers were used by the EAF as conversion trainers for pilots transitioning from British Meteors to the MiG-15 and MiG-17. The Midget has had a long career with the EAF and was not replaced until the late in the 1980s. Egyptian assembled Alpha Jets have replaced the Midget in the advanced training role. (S. Sharmy)

The 1956 Sinai War with Israel was a disaster for the Egyptian Air Force with many of its aircraft being destroyed on the ground by RAF, French or Israeli air strikes. Others, like this MiG-15bis, being inspected by Israeli technicians, were shot down in air combat. (IDF/AF)

Thanks to a three year arms-for-cotton agreement signed with Czechoslovakia on 27 September 1955, the Egyptian Air Force started to receive modern jet aircraft, including MiG-17F Fresco Cs. The first examples, shipped by sea and assembled in Egypt, carried the Green/White/Green national markings. (via Author)

provided for the delivery of a wide range of weapons including eighty-six MiG-15bis and MiG-17F fighters, thirty-nine Il-28 bombers, twenty Il-14M transports and twenty Avia C.11 (Yak 11) trainers. A large Czech and Soviet military mission was in Egypt while runways were strengthened and extended and the EAF re-organized. Both Britain and the U.S. became anxious at this new regional "super power" and both countries withdrew their credit to a World Bank sponsored project to build the Aswan High Dam on the Nile. Matters worsened when in July of 1956 Nasser nationalized the Suez Canal Company, intending to use its revenue to help fund the dam project.

This MiG-17F is painted in one of the many camouflage schemes carried by Egyptian Air Force aircraft over the years. The Red/White/Black roundel without stars and the Egyptian crest in the fin flash date this aircraft as post-1971, when the Confederation of Arab Republics (Egypt, Libya and Syria} was established. The aircraft is armed with Sakr rocket-rails under the wings and a bomb rack on the fuselage side. (USAF)

This MiG-15bis was salvaged by the IDF/AF and placed on display as a war memorial. The aircraft was shot down by IDF/AF figthters during one of the air battles of the 1956 war. (IDF/AF)

Besides the Soviet-built Il-28s, the EAF also received a number of Chinese-built copies designated the Harbin H-5. This camouflaged H-5 (serial 1733) was based at Kom Awshim airfield and was used for maritime surveillance missions over the Red Sea. (EAF)

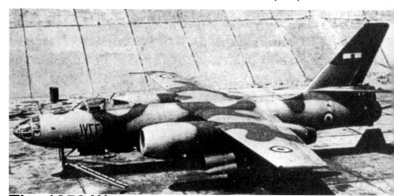

The 1956 War

The British and French, feeling robbed of their interests in the nationalized Suez Canal Company, had a valid claim against Egypt. Israel, on its part, wanted a war with Egypt. In a plan concocted by Britain, France and Israel, it was secretly planned that Israel should provoke a war across the Canal, and that British and French forces would "intervene" to protect their interests. An invasion of the Canal Zone was included in the plan, the RAF being detailed to bomb Egyptian airfields and destroy the EAF on the ground, while the French Air Force was to provide air defense of Israeli cities in case EAF bombers succeeded in taking off.

Israel launched its attack as scheduled on 19 October 1956 with three main military aims — the liberation of Sharm el-Sheik (blockaded since 1955), punitive action against Fedayeen camps in Gaza, and to deal Egypt in general a defeat which would discourage further threats. The IDF/AF possessed squadrons of Meteor F.8/NF.13s, Ouragans, Mystere IVAs, P-51Ds and Mosquito FB.6/TR.33s, with transport support provided by Noratlases and C-47s. This force was backed by a light attack unit with AT-6 Harvards, while Piper Cubs carried out liaison and light transport duties.

The EAF had eleven jet combat units: three with Vampire FB.52 fighterbombers at Fayid, Cairo West and Kasfareet, one with Meteor F.8/NF.13s for air defense at Fayid, four with MiG-15bis fighters at Abu Sueir, Almaza and Kabrit for interception/ground-attack; one with MiG-17F interceptors at Kabrit; and two at Cairo West with Il-28 jet bombers. The transport fleet was concentrated at Almaza and operated three squadrons with Il-14s, C-47s and C-46s.

Egyptian and USAF personnel look over an Egyptian Air Force F-6 Farmer fighter during one of the joint Egyptian/U.S. Bright Star exercises. The F-6 was a Chinese produced copy of the Soviet MiG-19S Farmer C fighter. The Egyptian Air Force received both Soviet and Chinese versions of the Farmer. There were still some seventy single seat F-6s remaining in service with the EAF as late as 1993. (USAF)

The Israeli Air Force started the war on 19 October 1956 with P-51D raids to disrupt communications in Sinai while C-47s, escorted by Meteor F.8s and Mystere IVAs, paradropped a battalion at Mitla Pass. The EAF was caught off guard and it was only the next day that Vampires were sent up on reconnaissance flights in Sinai while Meteor-escorted MiG15s began a series of attacks on Israeli columns which were moving towards the Canal by three routes, two across Sinai and one down the coast from Gaza.

Most Israeli Air Force combat aircraft participated in this all-out drive towards the Canal. Without doubt the Israeli Air Force would have fared much worse without direct French Air Force support, which enabled the release of all Israeli fighters from air defense of its cities to ground attack duties, and without the Anglo-French raids on Egyptian airfields which started on 31 October, crippling the EAF.

The Anglo-French-Israeli plan went as scheduled. Britain and France issued an ultimatum to both sides to withdraw ten miles on either side of the Canal. For Israel this was suitable, but the Egyptians could have hardly been expected to withdraw from their own territory, and that was what the ruse was all about. With the deadline expired, the Anglo-French forces unleashed their attack against Egypt. RAF Valiant and Canberra jet bombers carried out night attacks on eleven airfields with poor results, only fourteen EAF parked aircraft being destroyed. Day attacks by smaller fighter bombers followed the next day, British Navy Seahawks, Sea Venoms and Wyverns and French Navy F4U Corsairs flying off three British and two French aircraft carriers were more successful, destroying five MiG-15s, eight Il-28s and thirty other types on the ground.

The allied air forces raided all Egyptian airfields and by 6 November no less than 260 Egyptian aircraft were estimated to have been destroyed on the ground, practically annihilating the EAF. On a few occasions the EAF did put up a fight, but overwhelming numbers prevented it from becoming a real threat.

With the EAF eliminated, the Anglo-French forces effected their invasion on 5 November, but international opinion was against the whole affair, with even the U.S. threatening to intervene if the operation was not called off. The British ordered a halt to the operation and the French followed suit. Pressure from the U.S. forced Israel to withdraw from Sinai and Gaza while Egypt, although militarily broken, emerged as the political victor.

In an effort to lessen dependence on foreign supplies, Egypt sponsored a Spanish project in 1960 for a small Mach 1.5 fighter designated the HA-300. Named Helwan, the fighter made its first flight in March of 1964, but the 1967 war with Israel led to a postponement and then finally cancellation of the project. The HA-300 was the first combat aircraft to be developed in the Arab world and on the African continent and its continued development would have been an aviation milestone. (S. Sharmy)

Soviet Influence

The Soviet Union was quick to re-arm Egypt. Runways and aircraft were repaired, and supplies of MiG-15bis, MiG-17Fs and Il-28s began to arrive. Thousands of Warsaw Pact instructors arrived and by the end of 1957 some 120 MiG-17s and Il-28s had been delivered, with the EAF being reorganized along Soviet lines. In February of 1958 Nasser strengthened his position in the Arab world when the United Arab Republic was formed with Syria and Yemen. With this new confederation, the EAF became known as the UARAF. Even after the dissolution of the Union in 1963 Egypt continued to use this designation until 1967.

The UARAF continued to benefit from Soviet supplies, with new types entering service in 1960 being An-12B transports, MiG-17PF all-weather fighters, and Mi-1 and Mi-4 helicopters. During 1961 the air force was comprised of four Air Regiments (wings) of MiG-17F/PFs, one of Il-28 bombers and one with Il-14. One autonomous unit, thought to be wholly Soviet-manned, flew MiG-19s, while the MiG-15bis/UTIs were grouped into one large Operational Training Unit which had a secondary combat role. The forty-strong helicopter fleet was dispersed over several bases.

The aim of attacking Israel to retake lost territory had always been in the minds of Egyptian leaders. Moreover, the Soviet Union made sure

Although it carries UARAF insignia, this Tu-16 Badger F was flown by Soviet Air Force crews on Electronic Intellicence missions over the Mediterranean. The Egyptian markings were carried merely for political purposes. (USN)

A F-4J Phantom II of VF-102 aboard USS INDEPENDENCE escorts a Soviet flown UARAF marked Tu-16 Badger away from the carrier task force. (USN)

that the UARAF kept pace with the IDF/AF. When the latter contracted for seventy-two Mirage IIICJs during 1961, deliveries of MiG-21Fs to the UARAF started the next year to maintain the balance. By 1963 enough MiG-21Fs and the superior MiG-21F-13 had arrived to form the first Air Regiment, while the advanced medium Tupolev Tu-16 bomber was introduced into service.

From 1962 onward, Egypt involved itself in a bloody and long civil war in Yemen. Some 30,000 Egyptian troops and up to 100 MiG-15s and MiG-17s and twenty-thirty Il-28 were in Yemen for several years and were active in attacking royalist positions. A unit of Il-14 transports was heavily engaged in flying in supplies and ammunition to the large army and Nasser was only able to extricate himself from the situation after the defeat of Egypt by Israel in 1967.

The Six Day War - June 1967

The Syrians withdrew from the UAR during 1963, but in November of 1966 a comprehensive Common Defense Pact was signed under which Egypt had the right to station three squadrons of MiG-17F Frescos and MiG-19S Farmers in Syria. These aircraft deployed to Dumeyr. This, together with an increase in Al Fatah guerrilla raids and air clashes between Israeli and Syrian fighters, alerted Israel to a possible upcoming Arab attack on its territory. Tension intensified during April of 1967, Egypt once more occupying Sharm el-Shelk, closing the Straits of Tiran

This MiG-21PF Fishbed D (8040) is on display in the center of Cairo as a reminder of Egypt's long association with the Soviet Union. The aircraft was camouflaged in Sand and Brown uppersurfaces over Light Gray undersurfaces. Its only air-to-air armament consisted of two AA-2 Atoll AAMs. (S. Sharmy)

to Israeli shipping. On 30 May Jordan and Egypt signed a reciprocal defense agreement, being joined by Iraq on 4 June. On that day Egyptian and Iraqi troops and armor moved into positions in Jordan. For Israel this meant war.

During that period the UARAF was composed of two Air Regiments with more than 120 MiG-21F Fishbed Cs and E interceptors at El Arish, Bir Gifgafa, Abu Sueir, Fayid, Inchas and Hurghada. At Fayid, there was also a unit working up on the Su-7B Fitter A, thirty of which had just been delivered from the USSR. One Air Regiment (with four squadrons) was equipped with eighty MiG-19S interceptors at Jebel Libni, Bilbeis, Kabrit, Fayid and Hurghada. A large number of MiG-17Fs, augmented by a squadron of MiG-15bis fighters, was grouped into another four squadron Air Regiment for air defense and close support duties at Jebel Libni, Bir Thermada, Kabrit, El Mansoura and El Minya. Of these, three squadrons of MiG-17Fs and MiG19S Farmers had been detached to Dumeyr in Syria while another sixty aircraft, mainly MiG-15s/17s, Il-28s and Avia C.11s, were still in Yemen. The bomber element consisted of one Air Regiment of forty Il-28s and two squadrons with forty Tu-16s, concentrated at Cairo West, Helwan, Abu Sueir and Beni Suef. Two squadrons with seventy Il-14s, one with twenty An-12Bs and one with six to eight C-47s, operating mainly from Cairo International Airport and Almaza, made up the transport Air Regiment,

11

Ras Banas airfield at the start of the Six Day War with at least four Il-28 Beagle bombers at their dispersal parking. The gross lack of protection from aerial attack led to the EAF's virtual elimination during the first day of war. (IDF/AF)

Abu Sueir airfield was attacked by IDF/AF Mirage IIIs and Super Mysteres flying as part of the first wave on the early morning of 5 June 1967. This Israeli preemptive attack was the beginning the Six Day War. Four MiG-21Fs (probably of No 45 Squadron) were destroyed where they were parked on the concrete parking apron. (IDF/AF)

while a helicopter fleet for light transport, communications and casevac was available, composed of twenty-five Mi-4s, Mi-8s and Mi-6s, dispersed among several air bases and army stations.

The Syrian AF could field thirty-six MiG-21Fs and 100 MiG-15bis/MiG17F/PFs, while a small unit with Il-28 bombers was still forming. The Royal Jordanian Air Force was the best trained, although equipped with only twenty-one Hunter F.6/FR.6/F.73/T.66Bs. The Lebanese Air Force consisted of only twelve Hunter F.6/T.69s. Iraq did not share a frontier with Israel but had a substantial air force with some thirty Hunter F.6/F.59s, three units of MiG-21F/PFs, one of MiG-19S Farmers, two of MiG-17F/PFs and one each of Tu-16 and Il-28 bombers. The Algerian Air Force sent MiG-21s units.

The IDF/AF confronted this Arab force with seventy-two Mirage IIICJs, twenty-four Super Mysteres, sixty Mystere IVAs, forty Ouragans, twenty Vautour bombers and seventy CM-170 Magister armed trainers. But the IDF/AF was perhaps one of the best trained and most efficient in the world.

On the early morning of 5 June 1967 practically the entire Israeli air

combat force took off for attacks on ten Egyptian airfields. Runways were cratered, parked aircraft destroyed and buildings strafed in an attack that lasted some eighty minutes, while in the afternoon other airfields were bombed. By the end of the day, the Israelis claimed 240 UARAF aircraft destroyed, mostly on the ground, the element of surprise being almost total. Three MiG-21s managed to take off from Inches and shot down an Ouragan, while another brought down a Mystere IVA over Abu Sueir. On the first and second days of war Israeli aircraft also bombed airfields in Jordan where the entire Hunter force, except for one, was wiped out, in Iraq where twenty-three combat aircraft were destroyed, and in Syria which lost forty-three aircraft, mostly on the ground.

The Israeli army, supported by the armed Magisters and Noratlas transports, advanced into Sinai where some UARAF MiG-21s and Su-7s made attacks against Israeli columns, two of each type being shot down. By 6 June, the Algerian MiG-21 unit had arrived and went into action over Sinai. They were too late to prevent El Arish from falling into Israeli hands and were themselves captured when they landed at the airfield.

On the Jordanian front the Israeli army, backed by unopposed air sup-

The Egyptian Air Force received up to seventy Tupolev Tu-16 Badger bombers during the 1960s. During the 1967 Six Day War the Tu-16 fleet was based on airfields in Lower Egypt, particularly Cairo, where thirty were destroyed by the Israelis. EAF Tu-16s have been given a variety of roles, including level bombing, anti-shipping, missile carrier (such as this AS-5 Kelt armed Badger) and electronic reconnaissance. Some twenty-five Tu-16s remain in service. (EAF)

A MiG-21RF Fishbed-H (8502) reconnaissance fighter. Although configured for the reconnaissance mission with a three camera pack in place of the underfuselage GSh-23 gun pack, it carries AA-2 AAMs on the inboard wing pylons. This missile was a Soviet copy of the U.S. AIM-9B Sidewinder and remained the standard Egyptian AAM for many years. (S. Sharmy)

12

The Israeli lightning strike on Egyptian airfields on 5 June 1967 destroyed most of the UARAF on the ground, including seventeen of Su-7Bs at Fayid. The remainder were used for attacks against the advancing Israeli army in the Sinai on 8 June, with the loss of a further two aircraft. 7721 was a Su-7BMK Fitter A, it suffered from range and payload limitations, with four of hardpoints being used for drop tanks to increase its range at the expense of stores. The type saw further action during the October 1973 Yom Kippur War. (S. Sharmy)

The EAF was the first customer for the twenty-eight seat Commando, a land-based version of the Westland SeaKing, and received a total of twenty-eight Commando Mk 1s and Mk 2s between 1972 and 1974. The aircraft is operated by the EAF but employed by the Army for troop transport. (Rolls Royce)

The Su-20 was the export designation of the Su-17MK Fitter C ground attack fighter, a swing-wing development of the Su-7. The Su-20 carried no less than eight stores pylons. This Fitter C, 7771 of the Egyptian Air Force on display in Cairo, was armed with a UV-32 rocket pod containing thirty-two 57MM rockets on the forward port pylon. Other stores which could be carried included fuel tanks, GSh-23 cannon pods, a reconnaissance pod, iron bombs and AS-7 Kerry air-to-surface missiles. The Su-20 saw combat in the Yom Kippur War and was also used by the EAF during a five-day war with Libya during 1977. (S. Sharmy)

Western equipment, sought to replace Soviet types in the EAF, included two batches of six and fourteen C-130H Hercules transports ordered during 1976. SU-BAI/1277 was the ninth aircraft delivered, arriving during February of 1977. EAF C-130s are painted in a wrap-round camouflage of Earth/Light Sand with roundels above the wings and on the fuselage, but only one roundel carried on the lower starboard wing. (S. Bottaro)

After the initial six C-130H transports were delivered, a further order for fourteen was placed, followed by another batch of three serialed 1290/1292. EAF C-130s carried a Black radome on top of the fuselage just to the rear of the cockpit. With adequate numbers of C-130s on hand, the EAF retired the An-12Bs during 1982. (USN)

port, overran the West Bank, while in the north the Syrians limited their contribution to the war by long-range artillery fire. By 10 June, the day of the cease fire, with Israel in full control of the Golan Heights, the West Bank, the Gaza Strip and Sinai, the Arab Air Forces had lost 452 aircraft on the ground and in the air, of which 338 were Egyptian. Israel had lost forty-six aircraft.

Within two weeks of the end of the war re-supply of the UARAF by the Soviet Union began on a large scale, with some 100 combat aircraft being made available, mainly MiG-21s and MiG-19s. Since most aircraft lost in the war had been on the ground, the loss of qualified pilots was not serious. Two units with MiG-15s and Il-28s which had been stationed in Yemen were recalled and by the end of 1967, some 100 MiG-21s, fifty-sixty Su-7s, fifty MiG-19s and twenty Il-28s had been added to the inventory. Thousands of Soviet instructors, advisers and other technical personnel joined those already in Egypt, totaling 15,000 by the end of 1967. The Soviets, in an attempt to remove any blame of the war fiasco on their equipment, accused the Egyptians of disregarding Soviet advice on strategy and tactics. Soviet Air Force personnel took over control of a number of airfields and a five-year agreement was signed with Egypt which gave permission for Soviet Navy Il-38 maritime patrol aircraft to make regular sorties from Egyptian bases. After 1967, Soviet naval presence in the Mediterranean increased dramatically.

The War of Attrition

The 10 June 1967 cease fire brought an end to the war but not to skirmishes across the Canal, the east side of which was now occupied by the

This Mirage 5SDE carries high-visibility markings but, unlike other Egyptian Mirage versions, was equipped with an air intercept/fire control radar and was sometimes referred to as a Mirage IIISDE. EAF Mirages are based mainly at Tanta, where the OCU is located. A single squadron of Mirage 5SDR reconnaissance aircraft is based at Genaclis. (S. Sharmy)

Although lacking an all-weather radar, the Mirage 5E2s of the EAF are equipped with a SAGEM ULISS 81 inertial nav/attack system and a Thomson-CSF TMV 630 laser range-finder, making it an excellent strike aircraft. This pair of Mirage 5E2s of the EAF were on their delivery flight over the Mediterranean. The Black inner disc used for EAF Mirage roundels was larger than normal. (AMD-BA)

Israelis. The Soviets were against the resumption of Egyptian hostilities with Israel and supplied the former with defensive rather than offensive weapons. Requests for more Tu-16 bombers were ignored while large quantities of MiG-21 interceptors and SAMs were delivered, these forming a new Air Defense Command, separate from the Air Force of the Arab Republic of Egypt, as the air force became known in 1968.

In April of 1969 Egypt commenced a war of attrition which Nasser hoped would erode Israeli strength and morale. A number of dogfights took place between Mirages and MiG-21s, both sides publishing contradictory claims. On 20 July 1969, thirty Su-7Bs escorted by ten MiG-21s penetrated over sixty miles into Sinai where both sides claimed a number of aircraft shot down during the engagement. Throughout July and August such clashes were frequent and a particularly large air battle took place on 11 September when no less than 102 EAF fighters flew over the Sinai and were met by Israeli Hawk SAMs and fighters. The Israelis claiming eleven EAF aircraft shot down while the Egyptians claimed three for a loss of two EAF aircraft. The Israelis, who reacted by a series of successful strikes against SAM sites which were mushrooming all over Lower Egypt, were still superior in air combat but the EAF was gaining experience and becoming bolder. Israeli F-4E Phantoms made their first appearance in November of 1969 and began to be used on deep penetration raids into Egyptian territory from 1970 onwards. Often accompanied by A-4E Skyhawks, the F-4Es flew almost unperturbed over Egypt, both Israeli types being fitted with U.S.-made ECM pods which enabled them to evade Egyptian SA-2 missiles. Even the Soviets were alarmed at this fact (Soviet arms were then confronting U.S. arms on a large scale in Vietnam) and in early 1970 they took over Egypt's entire air defense organization. A mobile 'SAM box' over fifty miles long by sixteen miles wide was set up west of the Canal, equipped with SA-2s, SA3s and ZSU-23 radar-controlled AA guns. The Israelis carried out desperate raids against the box, but EAF fighters were scrambled to meet the F-4s and A-4s. The Egyptians almost invariably suffered more losses than the Israelis in these air battles.

In early April of 1970, the first MiG-21MFs for the EAF arrived in country. These were flown by Soviet Air Force pilots in the air defense role, and a total of five such squadrons were formed. It was the first time that Soviet aircrews had been committed in a war outside the Communist world and Israeli deep penetration raids halted abruptly on 17 April. Released from air defense responsibilities, the EAF renewed a series of air strikes into the Sinai with MiG-21Fs, Su-7Bs and Il-28s. Although being careful to evade meeting the Soviet-flown EAF MiGs, Israeli F-4s were responsible for shooting down four of them over the Gulf of Suez on 19 July. On 18 August 1970 a cease fire was agreed upon, Nasser's concept of an attrition of Israeli armaments having clearly failed because he had not taken into account U.S. preparedness to make good any losses suffered by Israel. Egyptian pilots, however, had gained valuable experience, confidence and, above all, had learned about their opponent's tactics.

The Yom Kippur War - 1973

Anwar Sadat, who had succeeded Nasser after his death, at once requested penetration aircraft such as Tu22s and MiG-23s from the Soviets and a small number of Floggers did arrive in late 1971, but these were air defense variants and they joined the Soviet controlled MiG-21MF units in the Air Defense Command. Sadat consolidated his position by defense pacts with Syria and Libya, but he was forming the opinion that Soviet support for Egypt in terms of arms supplies fell short of the amount of supplies furnished to the Israelis by the U.S. The Soviets' patronizing attitude towards Egyptians at all ranks and levels, the dilatory tactics practiced by the Soviets in arms supplies, and the Egyptians' almost total dependence on Soviet advice, were too much and in July of 1972 Sadat expelled most Soviet military advisors (some 21,000, together with their equipment), from Egypt. By this bold step, however, Sadat had not closed the door altogether to the Soviets. He only wanted to assert his independence from Moscow and wanted all decision-making, including that of going to war, to remain with the Egyptians. A slow trickle of military hardware soon started flowing again into Egypt, accompanied by a smaller number of advisors.

Sadat's aim was, nevertheless, a united Arab front for another war with Israel which he viewed as inevitable. Overtures to the U.S. after the expulsion of the Soviets were successful and through them he became closer to Saudi Arabia, Kuwait and the Gulf states.

In the afternoon of 6 October 1973, 222 EAF aircraft struck at Israeli airfields, communications centers, radar sites, SAM batteries, artillery positions and other military targets. The Israelis, taken completely by surprise, took some hours to react and sent waves of F-4s and A-4s on bombing raids across Suez. The Egyptian AA belt, now equipped with SA-6 SAMs, took a heavy toll of IDF/AF aircraft, thirty of which were shot down by the end of the first day. On the ground, the Egyptian army crossed the Canal in strength, with EAF fighters as top cover. Iraqi Air Force Hunters and Algerian Air Force Su-7s were active in the ground attack role, striking Israeli forces attempting to reach the canal. In air battles, the Israeli Air Force once more showed its superiority and EAF

Egypt ordered ten DHC-5D Buffalo transports in November of 1981 and deliveries were effected during 1982. Camouflaged in an Earth/Sand scheme, the EAF Buffalos are serialed 1161/SU-BFA to 1170/SU-BFJ. (G. Fassari)

An aircraft that never was! After having obtained U.S. Congress approval to purchase fifty Northrop F-5E/F fighters during 1978, Egypt cancelled the order because Saudi Arabia withdrew its financial backing. Some aircraft, like this F-5E (50606), were already painted in Egyptian markings and Green/Brown/Sand camouflage. Even before the cancellation, Egypt's President Sadat was skeptical about the F-5E, calling it a "tenth rate aircraft" when compared to the F-15s and F-16s then being delivered to Israel. Nevertheless, the F-5E would have been a useful aircraft for the EAF to effect its transition from Soviet equipment to modern U.S. types. (Northrop)

losses were also becoming heavy. Both sides, however, began receiving fresh equipment. The Soviets airlifted tanks and MiG-21s, while the U.S. delivered CH-53s, thirty-two F-4s and thirty-six A-4s by sea and tons of other equipment by air. As the Egyptian SAM belt was moved forward towards the Canal, air activity decreased but the ground war intensified and a major tank battle took place in the Sinai on 14 October. The next day the Israeli army forced an opening between the Egyptian Second and Third Armies and raced for the Canal, which it crossed despite of fierce Egyptian counter-attacks by land and air, the EAF being particularly heavily employed. The Israelis established a bridgehead across the Canal by 20 October, pouring in thousands of troops while F-4s, equipped with newly delivered ECM gear, managed to punch serious gaps in the Egyptian SAM belt. Without this protective cover Egyptian losses became heavier.

The EAF threw into battle all it had available against the Israeli bridgehead, including armed trainers and Mi-8 helicopters. In spite of a U.N. call for a cease fire on 22 October, the Israelis continued to push forward into Egypt proper, destroying military and airfields while the Egyptian Third Army lay completely cut off on the wrong side of the Canal. A second U.N. cease fire on 24 October was heeded by both sides.

The EAF had acquitted itself with honor during the war and, although helped by the initial element of surprise, had shown marked improvement over previous performances. As the effect of the SAM belt lessened during the final stages of the war, EAF losses rose dramatically, while Israeli casualties dropped proportionally. It should be said, however, that only timely U.S. supplies saved Israel from sure defeat in the air during the middle phase of the war. While the Egyptians were superior in SAMs, the Israelis were still ahead in close air combat. Total aircraft losses are estimated to be 115 Israeli and 242 Egyptian.

The Road to Peace

This derelict C-47 at the side of an Egyptian airfield was one of a few Dakotas which had seen service with the EAF after 1945. The REAF's No 4 Squadron had used the Dakota as a bomber during the 1948/49 war with Israel, dropping its bombs by rolling them out the side cargo door! (S. Sharmy)

Egyptian-Soviet relations improved immediately after the War and V-VS MiG-25R reconnaissance fighters reappeared on Egyptian airfields, flying high altitude missions over Israel. In 1974 small supplies of MiG-21MFs, six strike MiG-23BNs and the first of fifty Su-20 Fitters were delivered to the EAF, but Sadat was cautious not to become again fully dependent on Soviet supplies. That same year the first of several Westland Seakings and Commando helicopters (ordered in 1973) were delivered while a secret contract with Dassault produced the first of thirty-eight Saudi-funded Mirage 5SDEs and 5SDDs and forty-two SA342K Gazelles. Simultaneously, the EAF sounded out Western aero firms in an attempt to upgrade, with Western equipment, its large fleet of MiG-21s and Su-7s this process, however, taking no less than a decade to be realized.

Soviet reluctance to supply spares and replacement engines to the EAF, obviously generated by Egypt's outstanding debt with the USSR, rendered EAF equipment inoperable and forced Egypt to look for western equipment. Six C-130H transports were ordered from the U.S., followed during 1978/79 by a follow-on order for a further fourteen, of which two were ELINT configured. The EAF had to curtail its flying time on the MiG-21 and Su-7 and relations between Egypt and the USSR deteriorated to an extent that in March of 1976, Egypt abrogated the 1971 Treaty of Friendship and Cooperation. In the meantime a contract with Rolls-Royce enabled the overhaul of the MiG-21's Tumansky R-11 and R-13 engines, permitting the return to service of a number of fighters which supplemented fifty MiG-21s returned from the USSR (of the 150 sent there in 1975 for major overhaul).

Egypt was by then responding to U.S. invitations for a peace treaty with Israel, the Carter Administration being committed to this goal. This rapprochement with the Jewish State alienated Egypt's Arab friends, Saudi Arabia even withdrawing its financial backing for an Egyptian order of Northrop F-5E fighters which had to be canceled. Also relations with Libya, which had already been deteriorating for some time, broke down and in July of 1977 Libya attacked Egypt across the border with artillery fire. EAF Su-20s and MiG-21s returned the fire, bombing Libyan radar sites, villages, the LARAF Mirage base at Nasser Air Base and another airfield at Al Kufra. LARAF Mirages managed to attack Egyptian villages but all fighting ceased after five days, each side losing half a dozen aircraft. Egypt became further isolated in the Arab world when President Sadat made his historic visit to Israel the following November, which was ultimately to lead to the Camp David Accords of 1979.

One other longer-term effect of Egypt's peace with Israel was Arab

More for political than military reasons, thirty-four ex-USAF F-4E Phantoms, drawn from USAF reserve units, were supplied to the Egyptian Air Force during 1979. Serious serviceability problems restricted their use and in 1983 plans were made, but then withdrawn, to sell the aircraft to the Turkish Air Force. The Phantom's usefulness was demonstrated in May that year when the unit operating the F-4E, No 222 Tactical Fighter Brigade, was deployed from Cairo West to Aswan, near the border with Sudan, when that country felt threatened by a Libyan invasion. (McDonnell-Douglas)

The Peace Vector program, through which the first forty F-16s were delivered to the EAF was followed by Peace Vector II, III and IV under which no less than 174 F-16C/Ds were purchased by Egypt. More than forty this total is still to be delivered, but the type already forms the backbone of the EAF with bases at Beni Sueif, Inchas and Hurghada. Egyptian F-16s, like this F-16C, are finished in USAF camouflage consisting of shades of Grays. (General Dynamics)

withdrawal of financing the AOI. This was immediately replaced by the Egyptian Organization for Arms Production and priority was given to MiG-21 refurbishing. Peace, however, also brought with it benefits, in the form of U.S. arms supplies. Thirty-four refurbished exUSAF F-4E Phantoms entered service with the EAF in September of 1979, the Egyptian government also making a request for General Dynamics F-16 air superiority fighters. In 1979, China made a gift to Egypt of forty Shenyang F-6s (MiG-19S Farmers) which, although obsolete as interceptors, were suitable as rugged close-support fighters, and in fact another batch of forty was obtained later.

Training of EAF personnel on the F-16 started in 1980 at MacDill AFB while the EAF base at Ras Banes, on the Red Sea, was improved in anticipation of delivery of the fighters. The first F-16As arrived in Egypt in March of 1982 and by 1994, some 174 had been ordered or delivered, of which 127 are second generation F-16C/Ds. As part of an ambitious five year modernization program, five E-2C Hawkeyes were ordered from Grumman, these sales being facilitated by the close relations which had been fostered between Egypt and the U.S. Egypt made a number of air bases available to the U.S. Rapid Deployment Force for the Middle East and the EAF regularly took part in the BRIGHT STAR series of joint exercises with U.S. forces.

In the 1970s, negotiations had been held with France for the establishment of an advanced aero-industry in Egypt for the production under license of military helicopters and combat aircraft. The French/German Alpha Jet and the Aerospatiale Gazelle were considered and in January of 1981 the EAF signed for thirty Alpha jets, eight of which were MS.2 version with a nav/attack capability. Negotiations led to the assembly in Egypt of all but eight of that batch and all fifteen of a second batch ordered in 1982 as well as a larger number starting from 1984. A contract for the production of SA342L Gazelles was also finalized. Forty-eight Aero L-59E Albatros advanced trainers ordered from Czechoslovakia in 1991 have now been delivered and joined ten L 39Z0s already in service, these aircraft having been donated by Libya in 1990.

The program carried out at Helwan was expanded in 1982, to include production of some of the components for an order of twenty Mirage 2000EMs/BMs. A repeat order, placed in 1984, for twenty additional aircraft that were to be completely assembled at Helwan, had to be aborted because of funding problems. The Egyptian production line was also engaged, from 1985 onward, in the assembly of 134 Embraer EMB-312 Tucano basic trainers. The first eighty went to the Iraqi Air Force and these were followed by batches (totaling fifty-four aircraft) for the EAF. The Tucano partly replaced the Gomhouria in the basic training role.

In December of 1984 the first three SA-342L Gazelle helicopters for

the Egyptian Army were rolled out from Helwan. These aircraft were part of a batch of thirty and went into service along side the SA-342Ks that had been procured in 1975. Egypt also received large numbers (reportedly 100) Xian F-7 fighters (Chinese MiG-21F) for use in the advanced pilot training role (with a secondary air defense role). This program also included the assembly in Egypt of a substantial number of F-7s for the Iraqi Air Force (reportedly upwards of forty aircraft). EAF Xian F-7s were retrofitted with Western equipment, including AIM-9P Sidewinders, HUDs and avionics, the same as those fitted to the MiG-21MFs. The Su-20s were withdrawn from service during the mid-1980s, followed soon after by the Su-7s.

As a result of Egypt's support of the Coalition forces arrayed against Iraq during Operation DESERT SHIELD/DESERT STORM (1990/91), the U.S. agreed to sell Egypt twenty-four AH-64A anti-armor helicopters. With the collapse of Iraq, the EAF can be said to have regained a leadership position among Arab air forces, along side states such as Saudi Arabia.

IRAQ
Al Quwwat al Jawwiya al Iraqiya (Iraqi Air Force)

Iraq was the first Arab country to establish an air arm. After the First World War Britain gained a mandate over Mesopotamia, a territory beset with tribal rivalries, and the presence of RAF units was necessary to quell uprisings against the central government of King Feisal who, in 1921, was chosen as monarch of the new State of Iraq.

A national Royal Iraqi Army was organized with British assistance and in 1931 an air element was introduced. The first five pilots of the new Royal Iraqi Air Force (RIAF) underwent training at Cranwell, England, and flew the RIAF's first equipment, five DH.60M Gypsy Moths, from England to Hinaidi. These were formed into No 1 Squadron which was strengthened in 1932 by an additional four Moths. Three DH Puss Moths formed the nucleus of a second unit while a number of

The Royal Iraqi Air Force's first aircraft were all deHavilland products, the country benefiting from a twenty-five year treaty with Britain that had been concluded in 1932. In 1934, eight DH.84A Dragons were purchased and flown in formation from England to Iraq. Armed with three guns and capable of carrying sixteen, twenty pound bombs, the Dragons supported the Royal Iraqi Army and the resident British Royal Air Force in their suppression of insurgents. (Author)

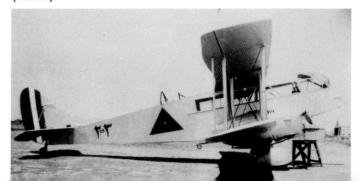

Hawker Nisrs equipped two other units. Relations with Britain were consolidated in a twenty-five year treaty of alliance in 1932 by which fifty Iraqi technicians were trained by the resident RAF unit in Baghdad and, in 1934, eight DH.84A Dragons were procured. Pilot training was entrusted to the RAF in Britain but three DH.82 Tiger Moths were purchased during 1934 to conduct pilot training in Iraq.

During 1937, five Savoia Marchetti SM 79B medium bombers and fifteen Breda Ba 65 assault fighters were bought from Italy, forming No 5 Squadron and fifteen Douglas DB-8A-4 attack bombers joined the RIAF during 1940. These purchases, which accompanied fifteen Gloster Gladiator biplane fighters and several Avro Anson light bombers from Britain, made the RIAF a well-balanced force with six operational squadrons and a sound training structure.

In 1941, a rebellion broke out among Army officers who, lured by Nazi Germany's promises of gold and military support, effected a coup against the King. German assistance amounted to the intervention of a few aircraft (He 111s and Bf 110s). The RAF, operating out of Habbanniya, inflicted a crushing defeat on the rebels, with the RIAF losing many of its aircraft.

The First Jets

Normal Anglo-Iraqi relations were resumed after the Second World

This Vampire T.55 trainer (serial 333) was one of six ordered during 1953 by the Iraqi Air Force together with twelve Vampire FB.52s fighter-bombers. These aircraft were used to equip No 5 Squadron at Rashid. All were camouflaged in a Dark Earth/Light Sand uppersurface scheme with Azure Blue undersurfaces. (deHavilland)

War. By 1947, RAF presence in Iraq had been decreased and policing the hilly country again fell on the RIAF, which that same year started to receive the first of thirty-two Hawker Fury fighters (including four two seat trainers). By 1953, three squadrons had become operational with the Fury. Oil revenues permitted Iraq to look for more modern aircraft and during 1953, twelve Vampire FB.52s and six Vampire T.55s were ordered to equip No 5 Squadron at Rashid, a second jet squadron was formed two years later. Between 1954 and 1956 nineteen of the more powerful DH Venom FB.1s and FB.50s were delivered, these going to No 6 Squadron at Habbanniya, the former RAF base having passed to full Iraqi control in 1956. In 1955 Iraq's pro-West attitude had earned it a U.S. donation of five F-86F Sabers.

The first Hawker Hunters received by the RIrAF were a gift of five F.6s from Britain delivered during 1957. These were soon followed by many more examples of the improved F.59 export version. This Hunter (579) was an ex-Belgian Air Force F.6. (Hawker Siddeley)

This Iraqi Hunter F.59B (serial 664) reconnaissance fighter carried a Red nose and vertical fin during 1965. It was previously flown as a F.6 (N259) with the Netherlands Air Force before being brought up to FR.10 standards. (Author)

In the early 1950s, the training fleet was re-equipped with DHC Chipmunk Mk.20s and ex-RAF Harvard IIBs. Hunting Provost T.53 basic trainers were used to equip the Rashid Flying College. A transport element was formed in 1953 with four Bristol 170 Freighter Mk.31Ms, seven DH Doves and what remained of the pre-war Avro Ansons, these aircraft equipping No 3 Squadron. The first helicopters, four Westland Dragonflies, joined the unit during 1954.

At first, Iraq remained aloof from the wave of Arab nationalism fostered by Egypt. In 1955, it joined METO (Middle East Treaty Organization), also known as the Baghdad Pact, and was rewarded in 1957 by a British donation of five Hawker Hunter F.6 interceptors. A further ten were funded through U.S. offshore procurement that same year. A training program for Iraqi pilots was established at the RAF Hunter OCU in Chivenor, England.

Dissent caused by mounting Arab nationalism in Iraq led to a bloody coup in Baghdad during July of 1958 which toppled the monarchy. Iraqi Air Force Hunters, flown by rebel pilots from Mosul, are believed to have been the first Hunters to see action when they attacked royalist strongholds in southern Iraq with cannon fire and rockets .

Post-revolution Iraq severed all ties with the West and moved towards the Soviets, who sent an advisory team to Iraq within weeks of the revolution, together with a number of MiG-15 fighters followed by ten MiG-15UTI trainers, eleven Il-28 bombers, fifteen Avia C-11 trainers, and a number of An-2 and Il-14 transports. Pilot and technical training was undertaken in both the USSR and Eastern Europe.

By 1962, the first examples of the supersonic MiG-19 and MiG-21 had been delivered. The air force, which after the revolution had been reorganized as the Iraqi Air Force (IrAF) consisted of twelve fully-equipped squadrons with a total strength of around 250 aircraft deployed mainly at Habbanniya, Rashid and Shaiba. Three interceptor squadrons were equipped with twelve MiG-21Fs, seventeen MiG-19s and seventeen MiG-17PFs respectively, while one fighter-bomber unit flew fourteen Venom FB.50s and twelve Vampire FB.52s, a third unit was still flying the Fury FB. 11. Two bomber squadrons were equipped with eleven Il-28s and ten Tu-16s respectively and the two transport units used a variety of aircraft including three Bristol 170s, eight An-12Bs, fourteen Il-14Ms, two Herons and two Doves. A mixed force of Mi-1s, Mi-4s and Dragonflies equipped the helicopter unit, while training aircraft, concentrated at the Flying College of Rashid, included DHC Chipmunk T.20s, Avia C-11s, Provost T.53s and two seat Furys. Advanced and conver-

After the revolution, Iraq continued to purchase British arms, especially Hawker Hunters. This Hunter (661) was an ex-Belgian Air Force F.6 refurbished by Hawker delivered to Iraq in October of 1966. The aircraft had a Red nose, wingtips and tail assembly. (Bob Elliot)

The Antonov An-12 was the Soviets' reply to the U.S. C-130 Hercules and was supplied to many of the USSR's client states. The Iraqi Air Force was believed to have received a total of eleven An-12B Cub As. This Cub was transiting through Luqa, Malta during the late 1960s. (Author)

Iraqi An-12Bs usually carried their serial on the forward fuselage below the I.A.F. legend and its Arabic equivalent at the mid-fuselage point near the national insignia. A construction number in very small digits was sometimes painted on the fin above the tailplane. (Author)

sion training as well as armament training was conducted with MiG-15bis/UTIs and Vampire T.55s.

The delivery of several reconditioned Hunters during the 1960s enabled the partial retirement of the MiG-17s. Arms deals with Britain continued and twelve Westland Wessex Mk.52 helicopters and twenty BAC Jet Provost T.52 light strike/trainers were ordered in 1963/64, but the USSR remained the main source of supply. Further MiG-21Fs and updated MiG-21PFs were delivered during 1966, permitting the re-equipment of three units with MiG-21 variants in 1967.

War with Israel

During the June 1967 Six Day War, Israeli Vautour bombers, escorted by Mirage IIIs, attacked H-3 airfield. They were intercepted by Iraqi MiG-21s and Hunters, the latter fairing surprisingly well against the Mirages. On 6 June the IrAF went on the offensive and dispatched four Tu-16 bombers from Habbanniya towards Israel. Only one eventually bombed its target and it was brought down over Ramat David by Mirages. The Israeli Air Force attacked H-3 again and also hit Habbanniya, destroying in all (on the ground and in the air) twelve MiG-21s, five Hunters, three Il-28s, one Tu-16 and two MiG-17s.

The USSR set in motion a major rearmament program for Arab air forces to make up for war losses. Iraq received MiG-21MFs, Su-7Bs, An-24 and An-26 transports and, from Czechoslovakia, L 29 Delfin jet trainers. Training on Hunters and MiG-21s was carried out in India from 1968 onwards. A second revolution occurred in Iraq during 1968 and relations with the RAF, which had started in 1931 were finally broken off.

A 1972 Friendship and Cooperation Agreement with the USSR covered the vast quantities of arms pouring into Iraq, including more MiG-21MFs (ninety in service by 1970), Su-7BMK ground attack fighters and Mi-8 helicopters. Under the terms of the agreement, the V-VS deployed a force of Tu-22 bombers to Baghdad, the first of its type to be seen in the Middle East.

Iraqi Air Force Tu-16 Badger Gs carried an unusual camouflage finish of Dark Brown over Sand with Light Gray undersurfaces. The aircraft saw action in the Iran/Iraq war, conducting raids against Iranian towns and villages.

In October of 1973 the Arabs launched a surprise attack on Israel and the IrAF was again in action. A squadron of Hunter F.59s was sent to Egypt, raiding Israeli positions across Suez from Egyptian bases. A squadron of MiG-21s and a squadron of Hunter F.59 fighters was deployed to Syria, attacking Israeli strongholds on the Golan Heights.

A period of internal political stability was created in Iraq after the Ba'ath Party revolution of 1968 and the availability of convertible currency from increasing oil revenues permitted Iraq to look for Western aircraft. After protracted negotiations, an arms-for-oil deal was made with France during 1977, under which thirty-six Mirage F.1EQs/F.1BQs were ordered, these being followed in 1980 by another order for twenty-four aircraft. Large orders for helicopters were also placed in France, ten Exocet missile armed SA321H Super Frelons, forty SA.316B Alouette IIIs, forty HOT missile armed SA.342K Gazelles and SA.330 Pumas. An arms deal with the Soviet Union in 1977 led to the delivery of MiG-23Bs, more MiG-21MFs and MiG-21PFMs, Su-20 Fitter Cs, Tu-22 bombers, further supplies of Su-7BMK Fitter As and fourteen Mi-6 helicopters.

By 1980, Iraq could boast of a complete 28,000 man and 340 aircraft

The Iraqi Revolution of 1958 opened the way for the Soviets. This overall Natural Metal MiG-17F Fresco C carries the early style fin flash used during the late 1950s. The aircraft carries its serial (452) in Black Arabic characters on the nose. Iraq received over 100 MiG-17Fs/PFs over the years, some remaining in service into the 1980s. (Via Author)

This An-12B Cub A carries the contractor number, 5910, on the fin below the fin flash. This aircraft was one of several Cubs transiting through Luqa, Malta during the 1968/69 period. The Cub remains the primary tactical transport of the Iraqi Air Force. (Author)

force. The Air Defense Command comprised five interceptor squadrons with a total of 115 MiG-21MF/21PFMs as well as an Army-manned air control and surveillance system coupled with SA-2, SA-3 and SA-6 SAM batteries.

Support Command included twelve ground-attack units, four with eighty MiG-23Bs, three with sixty Su-7BMKs, three with thirty Su-20s and two with the aging but still valuable Hunter F.59/59A/59Bs. Bomber and light strike units also formed part of Support Command, which had one unit equipped with eight Tu-16s and twelve Tu-22s as well as one squadron with obsolete Il-28s, light strike was confined to the remaining twelve old Jet Provost T.52s.

Transport Command was comprised of two squadrons with several different types, ten An-2s, eight An-12Bs, eight An-24s, two An-26s, thirteen Il-14Ms, two Herons and two Tu-124s, the IrAF was also the first foreign operator of the Il-76 long haul transport.

Training was still concentrated at Rashid, students starting on the Yak-18 and progressing to the Avia C-11, L 29 or L 39 Albatros. They then proceeded to the MiG-15UTI or L 39Z for armament training.

The Iraqi Air Force was the first non-European customer of the Aero L-39 Albatros, twenty-two of the L-39Z0 version being purchased during 1975 as replacements for the Aero L-29 Delfin. Later, during the 1976/85 period, an additional fifty-nine aircraft were purchased for the weapons training role. (Aero)

Iraq purchased twenty Jet Provost MK.52 armed jet trainers, serialed 600 through 619. The aircraft were overall natural metal with Dayglo-Red areas on the rear fuselage and Dayglo-Red stripes on wingtip tanks and wings. The Jet Provost was replaced by the Aero L-29 which was later replaced by the L-39. (Hunting Aircraft)

Conversion training to combat types was made at operational squadron level. In 1980, Pilatus PC-7s were introduced into the training cycle.

The helicopter fleet was organized around eight squadrons, which flew thirty-five Mi-4s, eighty Mi-8s, seven Wessex Mk.52s and three Pumas for transportation and assault, fourteen Mi-6s for heavy lift, forty anti-tank Gazelles, eight anti-ship Super Frelons, and forty-seven Alouette IIIs. During 1980, some forty-one Mi-24 Hind assault and anti-armor helicopters were introduced into the inventory, with further orders to follow.

War with Iran - 1980 - 1988

Iraq and Iran share a 910 mile frontier and border skirmishes were common, particularly along the southern frontier at the Shatt el-Arab waterway, which is important to Iraq because it is the country's only outlet to the sea. Both Iran and Iraq claimed both banks of the Shatt, but the Algiers Treaty of 1975 defined a mid-channel border which Iraq, then being in an inferior position with Iran, had to accept.

The fall of the Shah in 1978 plunged Iran into chaos. Iran lost its U.S. protection, the air force was purged of its best officers and most of its U.S.-produced aircraft were grounded due to a lack of spares. Iraq found its opportunity to even the score with Iran and, in 1980, abrogated the Algiers Treaty and invaded Iran, for what it thought to be the beginning of a short victorious war.

Although Iran had possessed a large and modern air force, low serviceability, spare parts shortages, the departure of the large U.S. training mission and the erosion of professionalism caused by the officer purges had rendered this force ineffective. It was estimated that only fifty F-4D Phantoms, sixty F-5Es and 200 helicopters were airworthy at the beginning of the war in September of 1980.

The IrAF staged an opening raid on 22 September against ten major Iranian air bases to immobilize the IRAF. The next day, however, the IRAF mounted a similar strike staged by a mixed force of 100 Phantoms and F-5Es, demonstrating that Iran could still hit back. This was followed by several raids and counter raids but few aerial combats took place. This was attributed to ineffective ground-control systems on both sides and a lack of air combat training.

Air support to ground troops was negligible during the first year of war, except for the helicopter forces — Iranian AH-lJ and Iraqi Mi-24 gunships. The air force acted independently of the army, with the result that road junctions and troop columns, normally easy air targets, were left unmolested. Strategic bombing planning was poor, but in December of 1980 Iraq made the first of countless attacks on Iranian oil installations on Kharg Island.

The Iran-Iraq War was mainly a ground war, with several intermittent stalemates interspersed with sudden eruptions of vicious fighting. The Iranian Air Force received a boost in 1981 when the solving of the American Embassy hostages crisis was tied to the release of embargoed military spare parts, enabling Iran to put into airworthy condition an increased number of Phantoms and F-5Es, these being the mainstay of the air force throughout the war.

The IrAF started to receive its order of Mirage F.IEQs and by the end

Iraq operated a number of different variants of the Mi-8 Hip assault helicopter. This damaged Hip was armed with a UB-32 rocket pod on the outrigger pylon. (USAF)

This Iraqi Air Force MiG-23BN Flogger has been modified with a refueling probe from a Mirage F.1 mounted on the nose at an offset angle. The probe was fixed and could not be retracted. (via Hans Stapfer)

of 1981 had a total of thirty-four in service. The Soviet Union had initially declared its neutrality in the war but started to shift its favor to Iraq and was reported to be supplying MiG-25 Foxbat fighters. On the ground, however, the Iranians were more successful and in 1982 regained most of the territory lost in the initial invasion and even invaded Iraq, on one front using paratroopers to secure a position. The initiative on land remained, for most periods of the war, with the Iranians, while the IrAF was superior to the Iranian Air Force due to the continuous supply of aircraft and spares from France and the Soviet Union.

In 1983, the IrAF ordered twenty-nine additional Mirage F.lEQ-5 armed with Exocet anti-ship missiles to counter Iranian naval superiority. Since this version of the Mirage could not become available for some years, the French agreed to loan Iraq five ex-Aeronavale Super Etendards, similarly armed, for a period of two years. The Super Etendards were delivered in October of 1983 and by the following year these aircraft were active in what became known as the "War of the Tankers."

In 1984, Iraq declared a "Naval Exclusion Zone" covering the mouth of Shatt el-Arab, and Super Etendards and Super Frelons, usually with Mirage F.lEQ top cover, attacked several tankers in the zone. Kharg Island was hit frequently, thirty-seven times in November of 1985 alone, becoming the most bombed target in the war. In 1985, the Iranians

declared their own "Naval Advice Zone", thus hoping to encourage shipping and reverse a situation in which their oil exports had been cut by almost half. But the delivery in 1986 of the Exocet-armed Mirages gave the Iraqis full air superiority over the Gulf. By late 1986, it was estimated that the Iranian Air Force had no more than seven F-14A Tomcats (minus radar/Phoenix capability), ten to fifteen F-5Es and about twenty Phantoms.

Substantial stocks of arms, including 2,000 TOW anti-tank missiles and 235 Hawk anti-aircraft missiles came covertly to Iran from the U.S. as part of an operation that was later to become known as Irangate (the secret barter of U.S. hostages held in Lebanon by Shia terrorists in exchange for arms). The Hawk missiles were influential in the gradual disappearance from the battlefield of Iraqi close-support aircraft, particularly after a MiG-25, two Tu-16s and a MiG-23 were brought down in January of 1987. The TOW anti-tank missiles gave a fresh impetus to the use of the Iranian AH-lJ Cobras.

The final year of the war saw an improvement in Iraq's professionalism and a decline in Iran's. More modern aircraft were introduced into the IrAF including MiG-29, Su-25s and Su-22s. In contrast, by 1988 the Iranian Air Force had deteriorated to twenty Phantoms, twenty F-5Es and seven to nine Tomcats in an airworthy condition. The Tomcats were involved in air combat, a very rare occurrence in the war, in February of 1988 when an Iraqi Mirage was shot down in a two against two engagement. As the last year of war wore on, Iraqi counter-offensives pushed the Iranians back, the land operations being supported by fighter and helicopter gunships. The initiative on land passed to the Iraqis. Iran was now hopelessly outclassed and outnumbered in the air and on the ground. Towards the end of the war, the Iraqis enjoyed a ten to one advantage in combat aircraft. Iran was nearing bankruptcy, its industrial base was smashed and on 8 August 1988, it accepted an Iraqi call for a cease fire.

The IrAF was a formidable force in 1989, with large numbers of Mirage F.1EQs, MiG-23MFs, MG-23BNs, MiG-21MFs, Su-20/22s, Su-25s, MiG-29s, MiG-25s and Su-24 bombers. In spite of having accumulated about $80 billion in international debt during the war, Iraq showed interest in obtaining the Mirage 2000, and negotiations were opened during 1989. Outstanding French debts, however, hindered progress and, in the event, no contract was concluded. As a result, Iraq began looking at the Soviet Su-27, but deliveries had not started before Iraq invaded Kuwait in August of 1990.

Operation Desert Storm

The West had viewed Saddam Hussein as a bulwark against Iranian radical fundamentalism and overlooked his sins, including his use of chemical warfare in attacks on the Kurds in 1988.

Successive Iraqi leaders had never accepted Kuwait's independence and had laid claim to that territory since Kuwait was established during 1961. Saddam's pretext for invading Kuwait in 1990 was threefold, he accused it of exceeding its OPEC quota of oil exports, he wanted $2.4

Iraq has always had a mix of Eastern and Western equipment in its inventory. This particular Mirage (4622) is a F.1EQ-6 of which sixteen were received. The F.1EQ6 carries an Agave radar and is capable of carrying AS.30 missiles, Matra 400 kg laser-guided bombs, and an associated system which permits it to also carry the Soviet AS-14 Kedge (X-29L) ASM. Iraq has received a total of 113 Mirage F.1 in a number of different variants, the type being based mainly at Qayarah West. During DESERT STORM, twenty-four Iraqi Mirages fled to Iran where they remain impounded. (G. Fassari)

This is all that remained of an Iraqi Air Force MiG-25 Foxbat after its hardened aircraft shelter (HAS) took a direct hit from a precision guided munition dropped from a Coalition attack aircraft during Operation DESERT STORM. (USAF)

billion from Kuwait for "stolen" oil siphoned off a common oil field straddling their countries and he wanted two Kuwaiti islands that control Iraq's access to the sea.

On 2 August 1990, some 50,000 Iraqi troops led by 300 tanks invaded Kuwait supported by Mi-24s, SA.342K Gazelles and MiG23s. They met no resistance from the Kuwaitis due to the speed of the invasion. The troops soon occupied Kuwait International Airport and the other air bases from which a number of Kuwait Air Force aircraft had managed to escape to Saudi Arabia. One Kuwaiti Mirage did put up a fight and shot down an Iraqi Gazelle but no other confirmed combat was recorded.

Fearing Saddam's intentions, an armada of air defense fighters and other combat aircraft from the U.S., Britain, France and other countries, including Arab states, were deployed to the area to liberate Kuwait and defend Saudi Arabia.

The IrAF's best aircraft consisted of forty-eight MiG-29s and twenty-four Su24s, both state-of-the-art Soviet aircraft. Iraqi pilots, however, had not completed training on these and had not reached operational status. The bulk of the first-line combat aircraft could not hope to face such fighters as the F-14s, F-15s, F-16s, F-18s, F-117s, Tornados and Mirage 2000s operated by the Coalition forces gathered in Saudi Arabia.

Iraq was given a deadline - 16 January 1991, to move out of Kuwait. When the deadline expired, large scale air attacks by the Coalition forces were mounted against military and strategic targets in occupied Kuwait and in Iraq itself. No less than fifty-four major and minor airfields being hit on the first day during which some 1,300 sorties were flown, half of them offensive attacks. By the end of the fourth week, 67,000 sorties had been made against Iraqi targets, for a loss of only twenty-eight Coalition aircraft in action and another twelve to accidents. Primary targets apart from airfields included Scud-B missile launchers, Iraqi Army installations, SAM sites and Republican Guard positions. The raids bottled up the Iraqi Air Force but the Scud B sites were more elusive and Iraq started using them on Israel and Saudi Arabia. Despite constant vigil by Coalition aircraft, no less than eighty missiles were fired between 17 January and 28 February.

On 26 January a large number of Iraqi combat and transport aircraft left their bases and flew at low level to Iran (which had remained neutral). It was later estimated that 148 aircraft reached the safety of Iran; four MiG-29s, twelve MiG-23s, twenty-four Mirage F.lEQs, four Su-20s, forty Su-22s, twenty-four Su-24s, seven Su-25s and fifteen Il-76s, the remaining eighteen aircraft being mostly civil airliners belonging to Iraqi Airways or seized from Kuwait Airways. Of the Il-76s that escaped, two or three may have been the Adnan-1 and Adnan-2 AWACS aircraft, an Iraqi modification of the Il-76.

By 24 February, the Iraqi Air Force and army were deemed incapable of combat and the land war was started by the Coalition ground forces. After that it took just 100 hours for the allied armies to liberate Kuwait.

The war against Iraq was undoubtedly the most effective air campaign in history and goes down on record as being the only war won from the air and the most one-sided war in the history of air warfare. The Iraqi Air Force rarely engaged in combat and when it did it was shot down. Allied fighters shot down thirty-four Iraqi aircraft without loss. A total of 110,000 sorties were flown by Coalition aircraft in thirty-nine days, an absolute record.

The 148 aircraft which fled to Iran were impounded by the Iranian government as part payment for reparations of the eight year Iran/Iraq war. Without friends, without oil revenues and without forthcoming creditors, Iraq will be hard put to rebuild its forces. Even if it does, this will now be done under the watchful eyes of its neighbors.

After the Kuwait failure, Saddam Hussein turned his attention to Kurds and Shia opponents in north and south Iraq respectively. U.S., British and French forces intervened, albeit belatedly, to prevent a massacre and established "no-fly zones" for Iraqi aircraft and SAMs north of the 36th and south of the 32nd parallels. IrAF fighters which entered the zone were shot down by USAF fighters. To convince Saddam to remove SAMs from the "no-fly zones", attacks on Iraq were mounted by USAF, RAF and French aircraft under a U.N. mandate.

At present, it is estimated that some 350 aircraft remain the IrAF inventory, more than half being combat types. Most of these are MiG-21s, MiG-23s, MiG-25s and MiG-29s and of these few are estimated to be fully operational.

Jordan took delivery of four Dove Mk IB and Mk 2Ds during in the 1950s, and went on to order two additional Mk 8 variants during 1965. This Mk 8 (serial 120) differed from earlier models in having slightly higher powered engines. Jordanian Doves were used for VIP transportation and King Hussein reportedly enjoyed flying these aircraft. (RJAF)

Jordan

Al Quwwat al Jawwiya al Malakiya al'Urdunlya (Royal Jordanian Air Force)

The air arm of the Kingdom of Jordan was established by the British in 1949 after the Arab-Israeli war under the title, Arab Legion Air Force (ALAF) with an ex-RAF DH Rapide. Its initial tasks were transport and liaison on behalf of the Arab Legion, Jordan's army.

The presence of an RAF mission, and the acquisition of a second Rapide improved the force. Prince Hussein was very aviation minded and formulated ALAF policy himself. The RAF mission stayed in Jordan not merely to administer the ALAF but also to teach Jordanians

This deHavilland Heron Mk 2D (serial 106) was one of two purchased by the RJAF during 1959. King Hussein often travelled in the Herons on short trips to nearby countries, flying the aircraft himself. On 10 November 1958, during one such flight to Cyprus, the Royal Heron (with the King at the controls) was harassed by Syrian Air Force MiG-17s, using the pretext that his aircraft had violated Syrian airspace. (de Havilland)

The Arab Legion Air Force, as the Royal Jordanian Air Force was originally known, received two ex-RAF Vampire T.55 jet trainers to allow the force to start a pilot training program under the supervision of British instructors. Aircraft 209, camouflaged in Dark Earth/Light Stone over Azure Blue, flies over the desert with King Hussein at the controls during 1956. (RJAF)

to fly. For this purpose, two DH Tiger Moths and four Percival Proctors were acquired. Artillery spotting was added to the tasks of the air arm and five Auster AOP.6 and two Autocrats were acquired in 1950 to form an AOP flight.

King Hussein of Jordan was, and still is, a qualified fighter pilot, earning his wings with the Royal Air Force. His flying instruction was entrusted to "Jock" Dagleish, a RAF instructor who flew with the King when he converted to the Vampire T.55. Dagleish, an RAF officer, was given the Jordanian rank of Colonel when he became the Commander-in-Chief of the Arab Legion Air Force. (Author)

In August of 1952, Hussein succeeded his father to the throne and as King was in a far better position to dictate matters within the ALAF. His aim was to establish an air combat element, but a lack of funds postponed his plans, and only two Auster J5F Aiglets, four DH Doves and six DHC Chipmunks were purchased during 1952. The King, however, learned to fly under the supervision of Commander "Jock" Dagleish, the British officer in charge of the ALAF. Later in his training he qualified on jet fighters. The training of Jordanian pilots and technicians was conducted in the United Kingdom at RAF establishments. Since funds precluded the purchase of large numbers of aircraft, emphasis was put on quality, an attribute which is still evident in today's Jordanian Air Force.

British influence was still evident not only as a result of a British subsidy and military presence in Jordan. The ALAF shared Amman airfield

After having received a gift of nine ex-RAF Vampire FB.9s from Britain during 1955, Jordan obtained further supplies of Vampires (nine ex-RAF FB.9s and seven Vampire FB.52s from Egypt). Three FB.9s of No 2 Squadron fly over the barren interior of Jordan carrying the checked flash and eagle squadron insignia on the nose and checkerboards on the booms and wingtips. (RJAF)

A Vampire FB. 9 of No 2 Squadron, Royal Jordanian Air Force. The aircraft appears to have carried standard RAF camouflage of Dark Green/Dark Sea Gray over Natural Metal undersurfaces. The checks were Red and White. (RJAF)

During the months following the Six Day War, the RJAF started receiving additional refurbished Hawker Hunters from Hawker to make up for losses suffered during the war. This Hunter F. 73, (serial 704/E, ex-RAF XF498) was a rebuilt F.6 that was delivered to Jordan during February of 1968. Most RJAF Hunters carried the No 1 Squadron wolf squadron badge on the nose. (Author)

(Right) By 1969, Hunter deliveries to the RJAF started to include aircraft that had been brought up to FGA.9 standards. One of these, designated an F.73A, was 828/I, an ex-RAF FGA.9 (XG237), delivered in July of 1969. Jordanian Hunters regularly staged through Luqa, Malta on their way to the Middle East. The Hunters equipped two squadrons, Nos 1 and 6 based at Amman and Mafraq respectively. (Author)

A total of four Hunter T.66B two-seat conversion trainers were delivered to Jordan. One of these, with the individual aircraft code B on the fin, taxies past RAF Canberras at Malta's Hal Far airfield during early 1969. (G.Mangion)

By 1963, the RJAF had some twenty-four Hawker Hunters on strength, including this FR.6 reconnaissance fighter (serial 712/N). The Hunter had full squadron markings on the nose, a Red fin, White wingtips and fuselage band and a Red/White checked rudder. (Author)

Jordanian and Iraqi Hunters were very often seen with Red nose, tail assembly and wing tips. This RJAF Hunter F.73 (serialed 709/K) was delivered to Amman on 1 October 1965, along with another similarly-painted aircraft (serial 705/F). 709 was a RAF Hunter F.6 (XF379) and was destroyed during the Six Day War with Israel in 1967. (Author)

This Hunter has had the rudder checkerboard painted out, but still carries a Red nose and White wingtips.

23

Four Douglas C-47 Dakotas are known to have seen service with the RJAF. This C-47 carries a Red/White checker flash on the nose with an antelope badge on the nose. C-47s remained in service until replaced by CASA C.212 Aviocars during 1975/76. (G.J. Kamp)

Funding problems led Jordan to abandon plans to purchase new Mirage IIIs or BAC Lightnings. This led to Jordan accepting a U.S. offer for a number of refurbished F-104A Starfighters. This F-104A (ex-Taiwanese Air Force) was delivered during 1966 and served with No 9 Squadron at Mafraq. (RJAF)

In 1965, the RJAF purchased four SA.316B Alouette III helicopters. Within a short time this number was increased to sixteen and the Alouette re-equipped No 7 squadron. Two camouflage schemes were carried, an overall Dark Green scheme and a three tone scheme of Dark Green/Sand/Tan over Light Gray undersurfaces. (RJAF)

with RAF squadrons, but also because King Hussein was Harrow-educated, Sandhurst-trained and had qualified as a pilot with the RAF. In fact, until well into the 1970s, the air arm was equipped almost exclusively with British types.

Transport and communications remained the ALAF's principal tasks, a Vickers Viking and a Handley-Page Marathon being obtained during 1953 and 1954. The following year King Hussein was informed that the British government would donate nine Vampire FB.9 jet fighter-bombers to the ALAF and two ex-RAF Vampire T.11 trainers were purchased for conversion training. Additionally, several RAF instructors were added to the ALAF for this purpose. The fighters arrived in

King Hussein was qualified to fly a number of different aircraft types, from jet fighters to helicopters. His favourite rotorcraft was the Alouette III. He often flew one to visit outlying settlements in the Jordanian countryside. (Via Author)

December of 1955, forming Jordan's first combat squadron. The jump from the Chipmunks to the Vampires was found to be too sudden, so ten ex-RAF Harvard T.2Bs were purchased for advanced training.

Jordan succumbed to Arab nationalism fostered by Egypt, and in 1955 Egypt donated three Gomhouria trainers to the ALAF. This relationship with Egypt improved during 1956, after the formation of a mutual defense pact between Jordan, Egypt, Syria and Saudi Arabia. This was followed by a gift of seven ex-Egyptian AF Vampire FB.52s later that same year. In view of its changed role and increased defensive responsibilities, the ALAF was renamed the Royal Jordanian Air Force (RJAF) during October of 1956.

Although it took no part in the 1956 Arab-Israeli war, Jordan abrogated its treaty with Britain after the Anglo-French invasion of Suez. The RAF advisory team was withdrawn and Jordan became dependent on its Arab neighbors, a mistake that was to be regretted when an attempted Egyptian/Syrian-inspired coup threatened King Hussein's throne during 1957. Relations with the West were improved again and twelve Hunter F.6 fighters were obtained in 1958 under U.S. offshore procurement.

In 1962, Jordan and Saudi Arabia agreed to unite their armed forces, the RJAF then becoming known as the Royal Arab Air Force. This was short-lived, however, and in 1963 the force resumed its former RJAF title.

The delivery of more Hunters from Britain made the type the backbone of the RJAF. The transport unit was strengthened in 1959/60 by two Airspeed Ambassadors and two DH Herons. By 1963, the RJAF had been consolidated into a small but compact force of twenty-seven Hunters, a dozen Vampires, a modest transport fleet, various Chipmunks and Harvards, and a new helicopter element which consisted of four

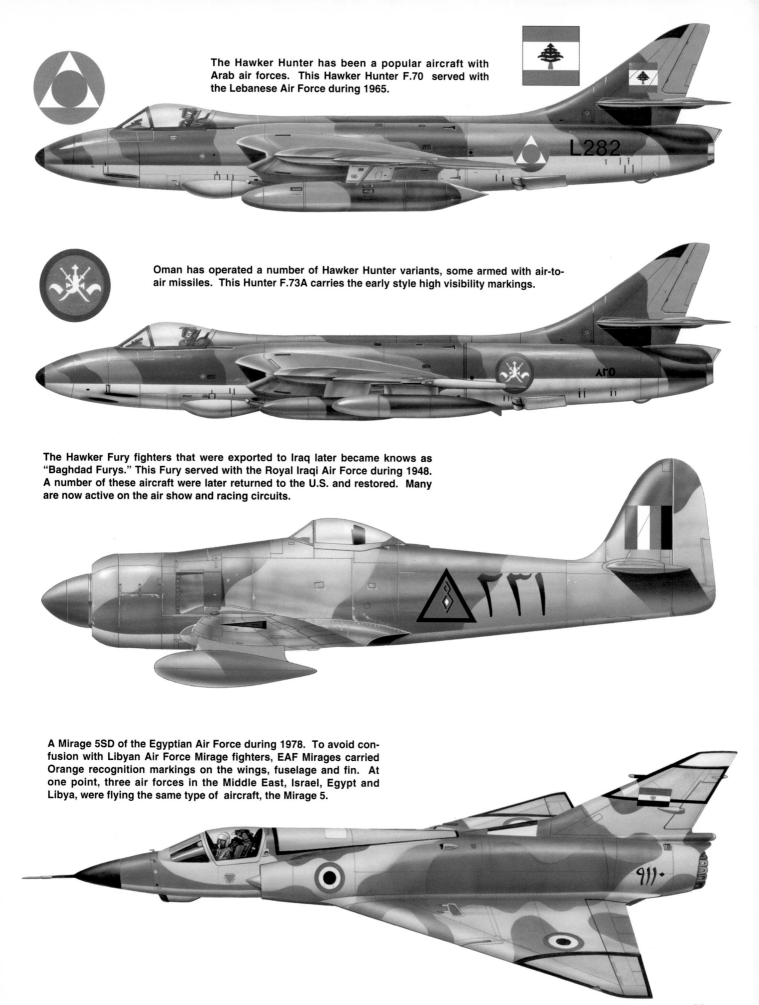

The Hawker Hunter has been a popular aircraft with Arab air forces. This Hawker Hunter F.70 served with the Lebanese Air Force during 1965.

L282

Oman has operated a number of Hawker Hunter variants, some armed with air-to-air missiles. This Hunter F.73A carries the early style high visibility markings.

The Hawker Fury fighters that were exported to Iraq later became knows as "Baghdad Furys." This Fury served with the Royal Iraqi Air Force during 1948. A number of these aircraft were later returned to the U.S. and restored. Many are now active on the air show and racing circuits.

A Mirage 5SD of the Egyptian Air Force during 1978. To avoid confusion with Libyan Air Force Mirage fighters, EAF Mirages carried Orange recognition markings on the wings, fuselage and fin. At one point, three air forces in the Middle East, Israel, Egypt and Libya, were flying the same type of aircraft, the Mirage 5.

Four ex-USAF C-l30Bs were donated to the RJAF under MAP in 1973 and 1976. They retained their Vietnam-type camouflage and were given RJAF serials 140-143. This C-130B (serial 140) had the serial in very small Arabic characters barely discernible on the extreme nose just to the rear of the radome. 142 and 143 were later sold to Singapore in 1977,while 140 and 141 were re-serialed 340 and 341 in 1979 and retained in service. (G.J. Kamp)

The RJAF contracted for fifty-five new F-5E and eight F-5F Tiger IIs with deliveries starting during 1975. These aircraft equipped No 17 Squadron at Prince Hassan Air Base, formerly known as airfield H-5. The F-5Es are configured for air superiority as well as having a strike role. Still carrying its U.S serial, this F-5E was eventually given a RJAF serial in the 900 or 1100 range, the first two digits indicating service with either No 9 or No 11 Squadron. (Northrop)

This F-5E (80-792) was part of a later batch ordered by Jordan. It carries the serial, 1151, in Arabic characters on the nose indicating its service with No 11 Squadron. Two RJAF F-5Es, 1151 and 1161, participated in the 1981 International Air Tatoo at Fairford, England. (Via Author)

Whirlwinds and one Widgeon, procured in 1958/60, and three Westland Scouts. In 1965, four SA.316B Alouette IIIs were purchased from France for AOP and liaison operations with the Army. This number was later increased to sixteen, while four second-hand C-47s were also obtained for general freight and troop transport. In 1966, the RJAF purchased thirty-six refurbished F-104A/B Starfighters which had been returned to the U.S. by the Taiwanese Air Force. A U.S. advisory mission together with two single-seat and three two-seat Starfighters arrived in Amman for the conversion training of Jordanian pilots in April of 1967.

The RJAF benefited from Saudi funding to purchase sixteen CASA C-101CC Aviojet advanced trainers from Spain during 1985. 1156 was delivered in 1987 and the Aviojet replaced the elderly Cessna T-37Bs of No 11 Squadron. RJAF Aviojets are equipped with a RWR and can mount ECM pods and chaff dispensers for the light strike role. Armed C-101CCs are used by No 6 Squadron for both training and light strike. (CASA)

On the eve of the June 1967 Six Day War, the RJAF consisted of No 1 Squadron with twenty-one Hunter F.6/FR.6/T.66Bs at Amman for interception/close support duties, No 2 Squadron at Mafraq with eight Vampire FB.9s/52s, a light transport and communications unit with Alouette III and Whirlwind helicopters, four C-47s and a small number of DH Doves at Amman and Mafraq and the new and untried No 9 Squadron also at Mafraq with F-104A Starfighters. Two days prior to the Six Day War, the U.S. mission and the F-104s, which were technically still U.S. property, evacuated to a U.S. base in Turkey. The Israeli pre-emptive attack on Arab air bases of 5 June resulted in the destruction of virtually the entire RJAF inventory, including most of the Hunters, five transports and three helicopters.

Once again Jordan turned to Britain for assistance to re-build it air force. A steady flow of Hunter F.73s and F.73As followed over the next three years during which a fresh U.S. offer for Starfighters, the number now reduced to eighteen single-seat and two two-seaters, was accepted. Contacts with the Pakistani Air Force resulted in the donation of four F-86F Sabers and the secondment of PAF instructors. In 1972, an agreement was reached with the U.S. for the purchase, under the Military Assistance Program, of twenty-two F-5E Tiger IIs as well as the second-hand procurement of three C-119Ks and two C-130Bs (all ex-USAF). The transports were delivered in 1973, while the F-5Es arrived in 1975. The previous year, the older of the Hunters were replaced by two squadrons formed with twenty F-5As and two F-5Bs acquired on indefinite loan from the Imperial Iranian Air Force after RJAF personnel had been sent to the U.S. for conversion training. The higher-powered F-5Es

26

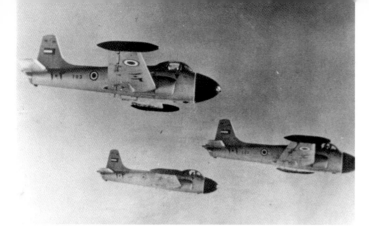

The Kuwaiti Air Force's first jet equipment consisted of six BAC Jet Provost T.51 armed trainers which were delivered in 1961. Three of these (serial 101,102 and 103) fly formation over Kuwait. The aircraft were overall Natural Metal with Royal Blue nose and tip tanks, while the fin, rudder and tailplanes were painted a Light Blue. (KAF)

were configured for air superiority, complementing the F-104s in the air defense role, while the older F-5As served in the close support role.

The RJAF did not involve itself in the 1973 Yom Kippur War and its expansion, although limited by funding problems, continued. More F-5As arrived from Iran, four CASA C-212A Aviocars replaced the C-47s while with Saudi financing further SAM batteries, eighteen Sikorsky S-76A helicopters and twenty-four additional F-5Es/Fs were acquired. Eventually, a total of seventy-three Tiger IIs were delivered. Eighteen Cessna T-37B/Cs were purchased during 1975 for advanced training, twenty Scottish Aviation Bulldogs being procured for the Royal Jordanian College of Aeronautics at Amman.

U.S. refusal to sell F-16 Fighting Falcons to Jordan compelled King Hussein to seek fighters elsewhere, and in 1979 an order was placed for thirty-four Mirage F.1CJ/EJ and two F.1BJs funded by Iraq and Saudi Arabia. The U.S. did approve the sale of four C-130H transports and twenty-four Bell AH-1F attack helicopters during 1979/1982 and 1985 respectively, while sixteen C-101 Aviojet advanced trainers were purchased from Spain to replace the T-37s.

Interest in the F-16 and in the ill-fated F-20 Tigershark was renewed during the mid-1980s but Israeli pressure caused the U.S. to disapprove the sale in 1986, ending what King Hussein termed "28 years of relationship with the U.S." The necessity of acquiring a modern high performance fighter forced the RJAF to consider several other avenues, but a fall in oil prices caused the Saudis to terminate financing and funding for such an expensive class of aircraft became a problem for Jordan. In the event, twelve Mirage 2000EJs/DJs were ordered from France during April of 1988 followed in September by an order for eight Tornado IDS variants, the latter order being rather short-lived owing to its indefinite postponement in 1989.

Relations between Jordan and Iraq were very close at that period and in mid-1990 a joint RJAF/IrAF Mirage F.1 squadron was formed at H-3 air base in Iraq. Iraqi fighters were often operating from Jordan, flying along the Israeli frontier during that year, evoking protests from Israel. When Iraq invaded Kuwait in August of 1990, Jordan was faced with a dilemma; Iraq was its closest ally, while the Coalition forces rallied against Saddam Hussein also consisted of some of Jordan's closest allies, France, Britain, Saudi Arabia, the Gulf sheikdoms. Forced by internal unrest, Palestinian residents, Jordanian fundamentalists, Iraqi sympathizers, King Hussein declined to join the Coalition and Jordan had to face the consequences for having lined up with Iraq, including the cancellation of the Mirage 2000 order in mid-1991, due to funding problems. The U.S. arms embargo has created spares shortages which grounded several C-130s and F-5s, while defense budgetary cutbacks resulted in some of these latter types being sold off to other air forces, five S-76As being disposed of as late as 1994.

Kuwait
Al Quwwat al Jawwiya al Kuwaitiya (Kuwait Air Force)

Kuwait, a sheikdom lying on the coast at the top of the Persian Gulf between Iraq and Saudi Arabia, was a British Protectorate since 1897. Oil production, which was started during 1946, has made the country rich, but at the same time a tempting target for aggression. During the 1950s, the Security Department of Kuwait was already operating two DH Doves, a DH Heron and a number of Auster single-engined types, although no official air force organization existed.

In June of 1961, the British Protectorate over Kuwait was terminated and Iraq claimed sovereignty over the territory, but quick British military intervention, including the deployment of RAF and Navy air units, deterred Iraqi aggression. In the following months the sheikdom, motivated by these events, decided to form an air force, with British technical assistance, as an extension of the Security Department. The Kuwaiti Air Force (KAF) was officially created with six BAC Jet Provost T.51 armed trainers and four Westland Whirlwind Helicopters, flown and maintained by British contract personnel. An RAF advisory mission was

The KAF received two DHC-4A Caribous during 1962 (serial KAF-C1 and KAF-C2). They were delivered in an overall Sand camouflage and were later re-serialed KAF 877 and 878. Still later, their serials were again changed to KAF 610 and 611. They were finally disposed of during 1979. (DHC)

The Hawker Hunter was in great demand in the Middle East. This Hunter T.67 (serial 219) of the Kuwaiti Air Force, was originally built as a single-seat F.6 for the Royal Netherlands Air Force and was later re-built with parts from G-9193, as a two-seater for the KAF. It was delivered in May of 1969 accompanied by two other Hunter trainers (218 and 220). (Author)

A MiG-15bis Fagot B of the Syrian Air Force during 1960. The aircraft carried the serial, 80, in Black Arabic numerals on the nose.

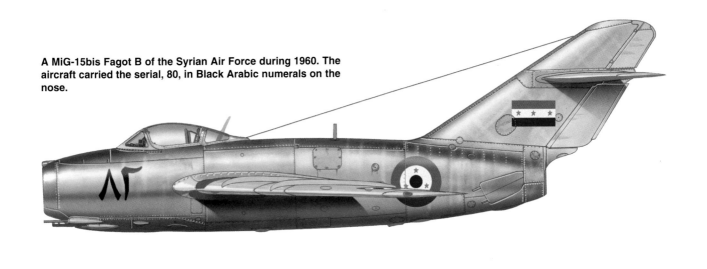

The MiG-17PF Fresco was the first all weather fighter to enter service with the Syrian Air Force. This camouflaged Fresco saw combat during the 1967 Arab/Israeli war.

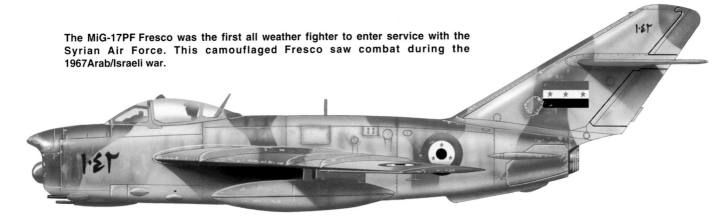

Iraq modified its MiG-23BN Flogger H fighter-bombers with refueling probes taken from Mirage F.1 fighters. These probes were bolt on, fixed units and were not retractable.

This Sudanese Air Force MiG-21MF Fishbed J carries the new national insignia adopted during 1983.

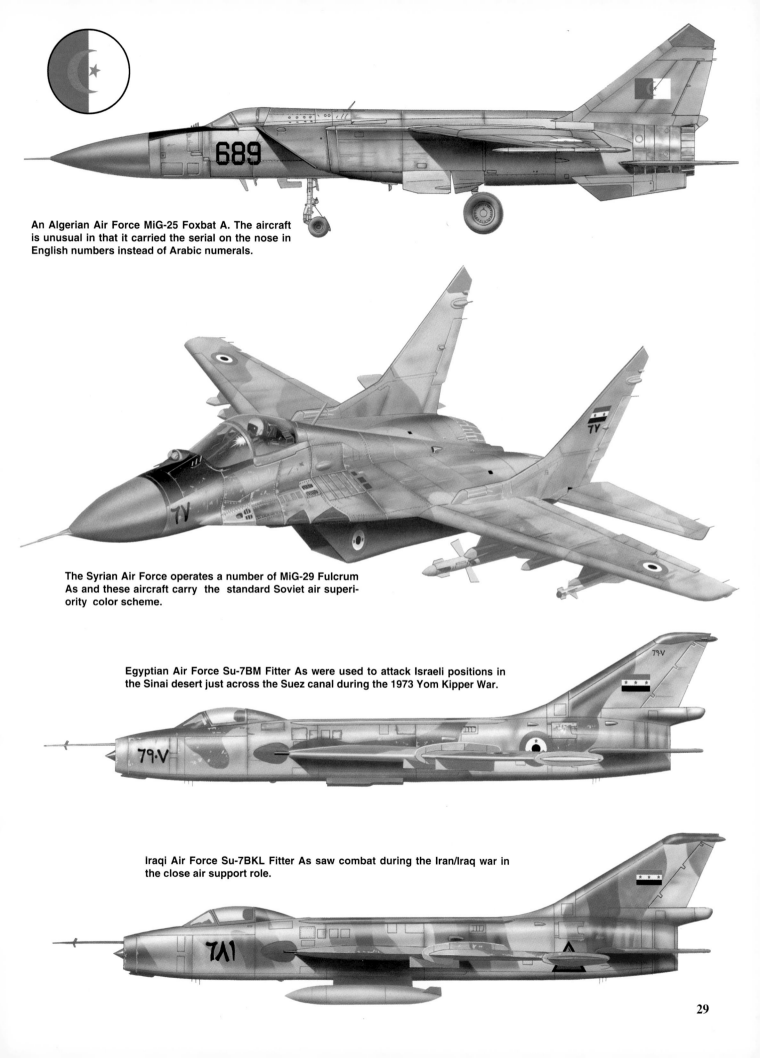

An Algerian Air Force MiG-25 Foxbat A. The aircraft is unusual in that it carried the serial on the nose in English numbers instead of Arabic numerals.

The Syrian Air Force operates a number of MiG-29 Fulcrum As and these aircraft carry the standard Soviet air superiority color scheme.

Egyptian Air Force Su-7BM Fitter As were used to attack Israeli positions in the Sinai desert just across the Suez canal during the 1973 Yom Kipper War.

Iraqi Air Force Su-7BKL Fitter As saw combat during the Iran/Iraq war in the close air support role.

29

Kuwait's Strikemasters were serialed 110-121 and coded A to M (with the letter I omitted). They were camouflaged but had their wingtip tanks painted Dayglo red. This Strikemaster (110/A) was delivered in March of 1970. Most Kuwaiti Strikemasters ended up with the Botswana Air Force after being retired from Kuwaiti service. (KAF)

also established in the country during that same year. Concurrently, a small number of Kuwaiti nationals were sent for flying and other training in the UK.

By 1964, four second-hand Hawker Hunter F.57s and two, two-seat Hunter T. 67s were added to the inventory while a transport element was formed with two DHC-4A Caribous. Hunter strength was increased to eleven aircraft by 1969, but at the same time a superior aircraft was being sought. The KAF selected the BAC Lightning F.53, and twelve were purchased during 1968 together with two Lightning T.55 trainers. That same year a contract was signed with BAC for the purchase of twelve Strikemaster Mk.83s which were delivered in 1969.

Military transport capacity was doubled in 1979 by the acquisition of an ex-RAF Argosy C.1, but the real improvement came later that year when the first of two Lockheed L-100-20 Hercules transports was purchased. The old Whirlwinds were replaced in 1968 by six AB-204Bs and AB-205As, which were procured from Italy.

The lack of an aviation technical foundation among Kuwaiti inhabitants proved to be a handicap in their use of the sophisticated Lightnings, and the rugged conditions under which the force operated was no help. The KAF therefore continued to rely on the simpler Hunters and Strikemasters and the question of obtaining a more modern type arose once again. Border skirmishes with Iraq in March of 1973 demonstrated the urgency of the matter, but it was April of 1974, after considering the F-5E, Jaguar and ex-USN F-8s, that the KAF decided to purchase eighteen Mirage F.1CK air defense fighters and two F.1BK trainers from France, the sales package included twenty-four HOT-equipped SA.342Ks and ten SA.330H Puma helicopters.

The ground-attack requirement was filled during 1974 when thirty Douglas A-4KU Skyhawks and six TA-4KU trainers were purchased, deliveries of which, however, did not start before 1977. To prepare for the Skyhawks, Kuwaiti personnel were trained in the U.S. under USN and USMC supervision. Training on the Mirages was undertaken in Kuwait itself by French and Pakistani instructors, while a program of airfield construction was launched with existing air strips being improved and equipped with Raytheon Improved Hawk SAM batteries.

This Kuwaiti Air Force Lightning F.53 was on display at the Paris Air Show prior to being delivered to Kuwait. The Lightning proved to be too sophisticated for the Kuwaiti Air Force and the aircraft did not have a long service career.

All eleven KAF Hunters, including the trainers, were camouflaged in Dark Earth/Light Stone uppersurfaces over Azure Blue undersurfaces. This Hunter F.57 (XE550) was in the process of being repainted in KAF markings, eventually becoming serial 216 in Kuwaiti service. It was written off sometime in 1971. (G.J. Kamp)

When the Iran/Iraq war broke out during 1980, Iran accused Kuwait of financially assisting Iraq, and Iranian fighters, mainly Phantoms, flew into Kuwaiti airspace on more than one occasion. In October of 1981, Iranian aircraft raided a Kuwaiti oil installation and during the eight year war Kuwait continuously felt in danger of being bombed by Iranian aircraft.

In 1980, the KAF represented a typically small but compact force composed of a unit at Ali Salim Sabah Air Base with Mirage F.1CKs which had replaced the Lightnings, the latter being put in storage or used as airfield decoys; two units equipped with A-4KU Skyhawks which had replaced the Hunters, these too going into storage; a light attack unit flying the remaining nine Strikemaster Mk.83s on close support and advanced training duties; a transport unit at Kuwait International Airport with two L-I00-20 Hercules, two Douglas DC-9 passenger/cargo aircraft (delivered in 1976) and twelve Pumas. Two units operated twelve SA.342K Gazelles each, one in the attack role equipped with HOT and the other for liaison, the AB-204s and AB-205s being withdrawn from service.

During 1983, a follow-on order for nine Mirage F.1CK-2s and four F.1BK-2s was placed with Dassault partly to make up for attrition and also to enable a second squadron to be formed. Six AS.332F Super Pumas, each armed with two AM.39 Exocet anti-ship missiles, were also ordered due to the troubled situation in the Gulf. By then four L-100-30 Hercules had been delivered, the remaining L-100-20 (one had crashed in 1980) was sold to standardize the force.

Training was a problem which the KAF had not yet tackled with success. Ahmed al-Jaber Air Base had been built to partly accommodate a flying training establishment, the organization of which was entrusted to McDonnell-Douglas in 1987 who drew up a curriculum based on the use of the BAe Hawk. Twelve Hawks were ordered in 1983, being delivered during 1985. As a lead in to the Hawk, sixteen Shorts-built Tucano T.52

Lying derelict, but complete, this Lightning F.53 (53-415/H) probably served as a decoy at Al Salem Sabah Air Base. The Lightning was one of twelve purchased in 1968, in addition to two Lightning T.55s. Capable of 1,500 mph and a phenomanal acceleration, the Lightning suffered from a lack of range and could only be used as a point defense fighter. (KAF)

Twelve SA.330H Puma helicopters (serials 551-562) were used by the KAF for liaison and troop transport. Camouflaged in Brown and Sand uppersurfaces over Light Blue undersurfaces, the Pumas were delivered in 1977/78. During 1983, the KAF ordered six navalized AS.330F Super Pumas armed with AM39 Exocet anti-ship missiles. (KAF)

turbo-prop trainers were ordered in 1989, these being fitted with provision for underwing stores to enable them to undertake secondary weapons training and light strike roles.

In spite of being a respectable force tasked with the defense of a relatively small country, the KAF did not respond positively when Iraqi forces invaded Kuwait on 2 August 1990. The Mirages at Ali Salim Sabah AB near the Iraqi border were surprisingly not on alert, although one Mirage did shoot down an Iraqi Gazelle helicopter. No other confirmed air combat has been reported.

After the liberation of Kuwait by Coalition forces, the KAF was reor-

Kuwait ordered a total of twenty-four Aerospatiale SA,342K Gazelle helicopters during 1974. This aircraft (serial 501) was the first to be delivered, arriving during 1977. The SA.342K version of the Gazelle was specially developed for "hot and dry" climates, Kuwait being the first country to operate this variant. Two basic color schemes were carried by KAF Gazelles: an overall Gray finish, observed carrying HOT missiletubes, and a camouflage scheme of Brown and Sand uppersurfaces over Light Blue undersurfaces. (KAF)

This Mirage F.1CK-2 (serial 722) was one of the second batch (719-727) delivered to the KAF for the air superiority role, and was camouflaged in an overall Light Gray. Mirage F.1s of the first batch were finished in a desert camouflage and carried serials 701-718. Kuwait also received six Mirage F.1BKs. The first two delivered, 719-720 were re-serialed 771-772, while the next four were numbered 773-776. (KAF)

ganized. The Skyhawks at Ahmed al-Jaber AB were expected to come to an end of their useful careers towards the early 1990s and in September of 1988 an order for thirty-two McDonnell Douglas F/A-18C and eight F/A-18D Hornets was placed for delivery during the 1991-93 period. The last Hornet was handed over in August of 1993 and Nos 9 and 24 Squadrons were equipped with the type. It also appears that Kuwait may be placing a follow-on contract for another forty aircraft. McDonnell-Douglas has agreed to take back the remaining Skyhawks in

(Above & Below) The Kuwaiti Air Force operated two DC-9-32CFs numbered 320 and 321 in the VIP transport role. Aircraft serial 321 carried two different schemes, one during 1986 and the second during 1989, the later scheme incorporated the royal crest on the fin, indicating it was part of the Royal Flight. (S. Bottaro)

The Kuwaiti Air Force purchased six Hercules transports, two of which were L-100-20s (serial 317/318 in 1971) and four of the lengthened L-100-30 version (serials 322-325 in 1983). This L-100-20, serial 317, crashed in September of 1980 while 318 was re-sold to Lockheed in May of 1983. 323, 324 and 325 escaped to Saudi Arabia during the Iraqi invasion in August 1990. (G.J. Kamp)

Twenty-four Polish PZL-104 Wilga four-seat liaison aircraft were supplied to the Egyptian Air Force during 1975 and based on airfields throughout the country. The aircraft in the background is a Czech-built Zlin Z526 trainer. The EAF received a few of these aircraft during 1982. It is camouflaged in a Dark Green/Sand scheme but no serial is visible. (Ake Soderlund)

The Algerian Air Force operated a total of thirteen Fokker F-27 Friendships. Eleven were Series 400M and two were Series 600 aircraft. This Series 400 (7T-VRW) carries only a fin flash to identify it as a military aircraft. Other F-27s carried roundels and the fin flash, while at least one was camouflaged. By the early 1980s, all the F.27s had been disposed of, their role being taken over by C-130 Hercules transports. (G. Fassari)

This Egyptian Air Force MiG-21MF Fishbed J (serial 8676) carries special recognition markings consisting of Orange panels outlined in Black on the fin, fuselage spine and wings. The MiG-21MF was the most numerous Fishbed variant to enter EAF service. The pylons mount four AIM-9P Sidewinders, indicating that the time period was after 1985, when the EAF MiG-21s were upgraded with Western equipment. (S. Sharmy)

Under a U.S. Military Assistance Program grant, three Fairchild C-119Ks were acquired by the Royal Jordanian Air Force during 1972. This C-119 (serial117) carries the logo Royal Jordanian Air Force on the forward fuselage in Arabic lettering and the serial on the boom just to the rear of the national insignia. The C-119's service career with the RJAF was rather short-lived, being replaced by the C-130 during the 1970s. The C-119s were operated from King Abdullah Air Base. (Author)

Painted in what became the standard Egyptian Air Force three tone upper surface camouflage scheme of Sand, Olive Green and Dark Earth over Light Gray undersurfaces, this MiG-17F (serial 2961) is displayed in the center of Cairo along with other aircraft and armor. An excellent ground-attack fighter, the MiG-17Fs in Egyptian service were modified with bomb racks on the forward fuselage and underwing mounts for rockets. In the hands of a good pilot, the MiG-17 was a tough dogfighter, as U.S. F-4 Phantom pilots in Vietnam found out. The aircraft in the background is a Su-20 Fitter C, which saw action during the Yom Kipper War of 1973. (S. Sharmy)

This Royal Jordanian Air Force Hunter F.73A (serial 825) was passing through Malta on its way back to Jordan after an overhaul in the U.K. during July of 1972. Hunters remained the backbone of the RJAF until replaced by Northrop F-5s in 1974. During 1975, Hunter 825 was donated to the Sultan of Oman Air Force. (G. Mangion)

In 1973/74 the Force Aerienne Libanaise purchased six Agusta Bell AB-212s, a militarized version of the Bell 212 constructed and marketed by Italy. L-251 was the first to be delivered, followed by 252-256. Another six serialed L-557-562 were purchased during 1979, and the first six were re-numbered L-551-556. L-560 was burned out in Beirut in August of 1982, while a few examples still remain in service today. (Author)

The Royal Libyan Air Force received eight of the sixteen F-5As and two F-5Bs ordered during 1968. The delivery enabled the RLAF to form a combat unit based at Whellus Air Base where U.S. personnel conducted conversion training for the Libyan pilots. The September 1969 revolt halted delivery of the second batch of eight F-5As. (Author)

Thirty-four Mirage F.1CJ and F.1EJ fighters and two F.1BJ trainers were ordered in 1979. This F.1EJ (serial 104) was assigned to No 1 Squadron and was optimized for the strike role. Mirage F.1CJs of No 25 Squadron are air superiority fighters and are painted overall Medium Gray. Funding for the RJAF Mirages came from Iraq which had to cease this financial backing when the Iran-Iraq war broke out. (G. Fassari)

A Mirage F.1EJ (serial 110) of the RJAF taxies out on a Jordanian airfield. During 1990, the RJAF and the Iraqi Air Force had very close relations and a mixed squadron of Mirage F.1s from both air forces operated from H-3 airfield in Iraq. (RJAF)

Six ex-USAF C-47Bs were donated to the Royal Libyan Air Force during 1963 and 1966. This C-47 (43-49217) carries the early Royal Libyan Air Force markings during 1968. Later it was remarked with Libyan Arab Air Force markings after the September 1969 revolution. (G. Mangion)

Twelve BAe Hawk Mk 64s (serials 140-151) were procured by the KAF during 1985. These aircraft replaced the earlier BAC Strikemasters in the training/light strike role and are camouflaged in Dark Earth and Sand uppersurfaces over Light Gray undersurfaces. (KAF)

This Lockheed L-100-30 Hercules (serial 322) of the Kuwaiti Air Force was hit by ground fire at Kuwait City airport during the Iraqi invasion and damaged. The L-100-30s were all painted in a Light Gray finish with a White fuselage top and a Red/White/Green cheat-line running from nose to tail. Kuwaiti Hercules transports are used for both military support and commercial operations. (KAF)

partial payment for the Hornets, while the fourteen surviving Mirage F.1s have been sold.

A UK-Kuwait defense cooperation agreement concluded during early 1992 may result in KAF orders for such British-built types, such as additional BAe Hawks and Shorts Tucanos. Interest has also been expressed in the Westland-built Sikorsky S-70.

Kuwait's geographical position and petroleum-based economy still make it a target for Iraq and although this menace may have been held at bay, an emerging Iran may be the direction to watch for any future threat to Kuwaiti independence.

Lebanon
Al Quwwat al jawwiya al Lubnanly, Force Aerienne Libanaise (Lebanese Air Force)

The recent history of Lebanon has been one of Muslim-Christian-Israeli-Syrian fighting which has destroyed the country and its armed forces, including its air force which was established in 1949 with two Percival Prentice T.1 trainers and a British training team.

Airfields were readily available in Lebanon, having been left intact by the French, who had occupied the country for many years. These bases included Beirut, Baalbek, Klayat and Rayak. The latter soon became the main base of the Force Aerienne Libanaise (FAeL), where RAF instruc-

tors trained Lebanese personnel. In 1950, the FAeL was enlarged with the delivery of eleven DHC Chipmunk T.30 trainers, a DH Dove and three Savoia-Marchetti SM.79s, the latter for transport and general communications. Six Harvard T.2B basic trainers were added during 1952, further batches bringing the total of this type up to sixteen by 1954, while further Chipmunks were also procured. A combat element was formed in 1953 with the delivery of four DH Vampire T.55 jet trainers and ten Vampire FB.52 jet fighter-bombers. This enabled Lebanon to form a combat unit the following year.

Civil unrest in 1958 led to the intervention of U.S. forces and to fore-stall further UAR influence, the U.S.extended its offshore arms procurement program to Lebanon, through which the FAeL received six Hawker Hunter F.6s. Six DH Tiger Moth biplane trainers were donated to the FAeL by Iraq during 1957, while a number of Harvards were made available in 1958 by Iraq and Syria.

A helicopter element was set up during 1961 with four Alouette IIs, followed in 1963-64 by five Alouette IIIs. The Hunter unit was brought up to squadron strength in 1965 when ten Hunter F.70s and three T.66C trainers were purchased, permitting the retirement of the Vampires. Jet training was enhanced during 1966 by the acquisition of four Fouga CM-170 Magisters.

The FAeL was seeking a fighter of superior performance to eventually replace the Hunter. In 1964, the U.S. Navy offered a choice of eighteen refurbished F-8 Crusaders or sixteen A-4B/C Skyhawks but the FAeL opted to buy new production Mirage IIIs, ten IIIEL fighters and two IIIBL trainers being ordered in 1965 together with fifteen Matra R.530 AAMs, all being delivered between September of 1967 and March of 1969. Lebanese pilots underwent training with the French Air Force at Istres. Once delivered, five of the Mirages were immediately put in storage while the rest were rarely used. In fact the FAeL's favorite fighter seems to have been the Hunter, six F.70s being ordered in 1975 although only three had been delivered before the civil war broke out. In 1973/74, six Agusta-Bell AB-212s had been purchased for army liaison.

The presence of thousands of PLO guerrillas in Lebanon destroyed the delicate ethnic and religious balance on which the Lebanese constitution was based, and Israeli raids on PLO camps in the country increased ten-

The KAF purchased thirty-six A-4KU Skyhawks, including six TA-4KUs, to replace the Hunters in the ground attack role. The aircraft were all new production and based on the A-4M. They were delivered camouflaged in a camouflage of Dark Earth and Sand uppersurfaces over Light Blue undersurfaces. KAF A-4s were serialed 801-830 (A4KUs) and 881-886 (TA-4KUs). (KAF)

Forty F/A-18 Hornets were contracted for by the KAF during 1988, deliveries starting in January of 1992. The order also included 200 Sparrow and 120 Sidewinder AAMs, 300 Maverick missiles and 200 cluster bombs. These F/A-18s are the first to be powered by the F404-GE-402 engine, and are serialed 441-448 (F/A-18Ds) while the F/A-18Cs start with serial 401. (KAF)

Eleven Chipmunk T.30s were acquired by the Lebanese Air Force from Canada during 1950. These were augmented by further Chipmunk T.20s from Britain during 1954. They were delivered to Rayak where RAF instructors trained Lebanese pilots. (Via Author)

The first jet equipment and combat aircraft for the Lebanese Air Force was the DH Vampire, a unit forming at Kleyate during 1953, which included three Vampire T.55 trainers. This Lebanese Air Force DH Vampire T.55 shares the ramp at a European air show with an Israeli EL AL Airlines Bristol Britannia. The aircraft's serial, L160, was painted on a Yellow band around the tail booms. The wings had similar bands. (C.J. Damato)

sion. Beirut became a battlefield between Christian against Muslim and Druze militias. Use of the multi-faction Lebanese Army led to the latter's gradual disintegration and in June of 1976 Syrian troops invaded Lebanon in anticipation of an Israeli invasion. The Hunter unit flew some sorties in support of Syrian troops endeavoring to restore order, but most FAeL activity at this stage was carried out by helicopters on communications and army liaison. Order was restored by October and an Arab peace-keeping force, predominantly Syrian, remained in the country.

Before the fighting had broken out, the FAeL had added another batch of Fouga Magisters and six Scottish Aviation Bulldogs to its training establishment, and was looking for a suitable aircraft to replace both the little-used Mirages and the much-used Hunters, but the search was interrupted by the civil war, attention being given instead to rotary types for the army. In 1979, six additional AB-212s, twelve SA.330L Pumas and seven SA.342 Gazelles were ordered as part of an Army re-equipment program, all were delivered during 1980.

In 1982, the Israelis invaded the country, preceded by IDF/AF attacks on Syrian SAM sites and aircraft based in Lebanon, and advanced on Beirut, occupying the western quarter. In the meantime, fighting, which broke out among factions of the PLO, and the siding of the remnants of the Lebanese army with the Christian Phalangists against Druze militiamen, added to the confusion. The FAeL did make an appearance in the

Summer of 1983, attacking Druze positions with the loss of four aircraft within two weeks. By 1984, the Lebanese official armed forces had broken up into their various factions, while Syrian and Israeli forces remained in occupation of their respective parts of Lebanon.

Given this situation, it is hardly surprising that expansion of the FAeL was nil. Indeed, the armed forces as an organization ceased to exist and the air force could not be considered as an effective fighting force.

It was only in November of 1990 that the Christian militia surrendered its positions to the Syrian-backed government and a reorganized official army. All other militias, including the pro-Syrian Shia and pro-Iran Hezbollah militias, as well as the Druze militia, agreed to withdraw from Beirut in return for cabinet portfolios in a new unity government. Meanwhile, the Syrians have not abandoned their historical ambition of "a greater Syria" which would include Lebanon, whose independence they have never formally accepted. Indeed, a cooperation agreement signed by the two countries in June of 1991 was considered by Israel as tantamount to an annexation of Lebanon by Syria. Israeli air raids on alleged PLO positions followed, but by July the Lebanese Army had asserted its authority over most of southern Lebanon where PLO camps abounded. The PLO had lost much sympathy the previous year when it supported Iraq's invasion of Kuwait.

Lebanon will have to rebuild its cities and towns before it can start thinking of rebuilding its air force and it may be several years before any substantial new combat equipment will be seen with Lebanese Air Force markings.

The Lebanese Air Force purchased twelve Mirage III fighters during 1967 (ten Mirage IIIEL fighters and two Mirage IIIBL trainers). These aircraft were rarely used and spent most of their service careers in storage while a civil war raged on in Lebanon. (AMD-BA)

Nine Super Frelons were purchased by Libya in 1971. It is believed that these aircraft were operated by the LARAF on behalf of the Libyan Army, the Super Frelons were used in the SAR role, operating over both desert and sea. This SA.321M Super Frelon is camouflaged in Dark Green over Light Earth. (Author)

Both the Libyan Army and Libyan Air Force operate Alouette IIIs in the liaison and training roles. The army procured a total of thirteen which appeared in at least two color schemes, the camouflage version being painted in a Green/Tan/Purple-Gray scheme with Light Blue undersurfaces and carries a roundel on each side of the cabin. (J. Visanich)

In 1981 the first Ilyushin Il-76M Candid heavy transports, similar to the U.S. C-141 Starlifter, were delivered to the LAJAF. The Il-76Ms were followed by IL-76TDs, both types being operated alternately by the LAJAF and the government owned airline for arms transfers. (S.Bottaro)

The projected Moroccan purchase of six Meridionali-built Vertol CH-47C Chinooks from Italy was not approved by the U.S. Congress because Morocco would not pledge to refrain from using the machines in the Western Sahara against the Polisario insurgents. In a major policy reversal, U.S. approval was finally given during 1979 and twleve Chinooks were eventually purchased. (Author)

(Left) Moroccan C-130s are based principally at Kenitra, and deployed to forward air strips with troops and equipment during the war with the Polisario in the Western Sahara. CNA-OS, a KC-130H, was one of nineteen C-130s purchased by the Moroccan AF. (S. Bottaro)

Twenty-five BAC 167 Strikemaster Mk.82s and 82As were procured by the Omani Air Force from 1968 to 1976 (serialed 401 to 425). These aircraft saw combat against the Dhofari rebels until 1975 when the insurgency was beaten. Equipping No 1 Squadron, the Strikemasters were replaced by Jaguars beginning in 1976. At least five Omani Strikemasters, including this aircraft, serial 404, were sold to Singapore in 1977. (BAe)

Libyan Mirage F.1s were often encountered over the Med by U.S. Navy fighters. This F.1 was intercepted by F-14As of VF-41 off USS NIMITZ on 18 August 1981. (USN)

Eight BN-2A-21 Defenders were delivered to the SOAF between August of 1974 and April of 1975, replacing the DHC Beaver. Some of the Defenders equipped No 5 Squadron at Seeb until withdrawn. Six have been sold in the U.S. (Author)

The first two of the five Airtec CN-235s that entered RSAF in service in February of 1987 were delivered in overall White with Green trim. Aircraft 118 is one of two fitted as a personnel transport. (CASA)

Although all five CN-235s operate out of Riyadh, three are dual passenger/freighters with folding seats and a roller track floor for pallets. These are camouflaged in a three-tone Sand/Dark Earth/Olive Green scheme. (CASA)

(Right) The growing tension between Libya and Tunisia led the Tunisian Air Force to purchase two C-130H transports during 1980 to enhance their capability to rapidly move troops around the country. Both aircraft were delivered in March of 1985 in an overall Medium Green camouflage. (S. Muscat)

As part of a modernization program started in the mid-1970s, the Mauritanian Islamic Air Force purchased nine BN-2A-21 Defenders which were armed with rockets and gun pods for use against Polisario guerrillas in the Western Sahara. Three Defenders are known to have been written off. (BN Historians)

Six ex-USAF C-47Bs were donated to the Royal Libyan AF during 1963 and 1966. This C-47B carries Royal Libyan Air Force markings, with the legend on the fuselage top in Arabic and on the fin in English. (G. Mangion)

Libya

Al Quwwat al Jawwiya al Jamahariya al Arabiye al Libiyya (Libyan Arab Jamahariya Air Force)

Italy had occupied Libya during 1912, but after the Italian defeat in the Second World War, Libya came under British and French rule. A U.N. decision during 1951 granted independence and the United Kingdom of Libya was formed that December. Britain immediately signed a twenty year treaty of friendship and alliance with Libya, extending financial assistance in return for the continued use of military facilities, including airfields at Idris el Awal and El Adem. In 1954, a defense agreement

The Royal Libyan Air Force ordered a total of sixteen F-5A Freedom Fighters and two F-5B trainer variants. Initially, eight F-5As and two F-5Bs were delivered to Wheelus Air Base during 1968/69. Libyan aircrews were trained by U.S. instructors first on the Lockheed T-33 then progressing into the F-5B. (Author)

An F-5A of the Royal Libyan Air Force lands at Wheelus Air Base during the late 1960s. The revolt of 1969 cancelled the remaining eight F-5As on the Libyan order and the aircraft were never delivered. (Author)

(Above/Below) Royal Libyan Air Force F-5s were overall Natural Metal with Red/Black/Green roundels and a fin flash that represented the national flag. The legend, Royal Libyan Air Force, was carrried on the nose in Arabic and on the fin in English. (Author)

with the U.S. gave the USAF the right to use military facilities, including Wheelus Air Base and the AL-Watiyah bombing range, until 1970.

Two ex-RAF Auster AOP.5s were donated in 1959, the same year in which Egypt made a gift of two Gomhouria trainers, to the Libyan Army air arm, which was created at Idris el Awal. Two Bell 47Js arrived from the U.S. during 1962, while France donated three Sud SE.3131 Alouette IIs.

For some time, the F-5As of the Royal Libyan Air Force were flown by U. S. pilots, since no Libyan crews had completed training on the fighters. The F-5s were eventually given to the Turkish Air Force (after a short period of operations with the Pakistani Air Force). (Author)

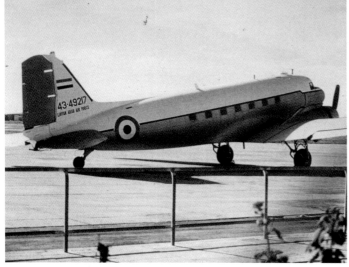

This C-47 (43-49217) carries Libyan Arab Air Force markings, which came into use after the September 1969 revolution. (G. Mangion)

Despite the discovery of large oil deposits, Libya made no effort to expand its air arm until 1963 when the U.S. offered to train Libyan personnel on Lockheed T-33As at Wheelus, two of these aircraft and a C-47B being transferred to the Royal Libyan Air Force (RLAF). In 1965/66, five additional C-47s and a third T-33A were donated to the RLAF by the USAF.

The imminent withdrawal of British and U.S. forces spurred the monarchy to set up a mobile air defense system, established by BAC contract personnel during 1968, while sixteen Northrop F-5A/Bs were ordered, seven being delivered by 1969. These formed a unit at Wheelus where U.S. personnel commenced training courses for Libyan pilots on the F-5. That September an army coup ousted the monarchy and set up a republic under Captain Gaddafi, the air force then becoming known as the Libyan Arab Air Force (LARAF). The new regime at once demonstrated its anti-Western inclinations. The remaining nine F-5A/Bs were not delivered while BAC's air defense network contract was cancelled and early evacuation dates for British and U. S. forces negoti-

No less than 110 Mirage 5s were ordered by the new Libyan regime during 1970, the order comprising interceptors, strike fighters, reconnaissance aircraft and conversion trainers. Their delivery caused quite a stir when it became known that some of the aircraft were loaned to Egypt during the 1973 Yom Kipper War. This Mirage (404) is a Mirage 5D (serial range 401-453) and is finished in the Dark Green, Medium Green and Sand camouflage carried by all Libyan Mirages. (AMD-BA)

ated, the former leaving El Adem and other areas in March of 1970 and the U.S. departing Wheelus the following June. El Adem was renamed Nasser Air Base and Wheelus became Okba bin Nafi, while an Egyptian training mission was invited to Tripoli.

Rearmament was high on the priority list of the new regime and in January of 1970, 110 Mirage 5s were ordered from France, Libyan pilots were sent to train at French bases although their progress was painfully slow. Nine SA.321M Super Frelons, ten SA.316B Alouette IIIs and twelve ex-French Air Force Fouga CM-170 Magisters were also ordered from France. In 1970, an order for sixteen C-130H Hercules transports was approved by the U.S. The French sale of Mirages to Libya had caused an international controversy, which was exacerbated when it became known that thirty-eight of the aircraft had participated on the side of Egypt during the 1973 Yom Kippur War with Israel. This, and the Arab oil embargo which followed the war, caused the U.S. to halt the delivery of the remaining eight C-130s. The absence of U.S. training facilities at Wheelus forced the Libyans to look elsewhere for flying instruction and in 1971 a Pakistani Air Force mission arrived in the country, the contingent being greatly increased during 1973 after deteriorating relations between Libya and Egypt led Egypt to withdraw its training mission from Libya.

(Above/Below) Nine Super Frelon SA.321Ms were purchased by Libya in 1971. Thought to have been operated by the LARAF on behalf of the Libyan Army, the Super Frelons were used in the SAR role, operating over both desert and sea. The type of camouflage worn by Libyan Super Frelons with serials in the LC-150 range was a Dark Green and Dark Purple Gray pattern applied over Light Earth, with Light Blue undersurfaces. (Author/J. Visanich)

The Libyan Navy received at least six SA.321GM Super Frelons (serials LC-193-195 and LC-202-204). They carried the standard French Navy scheme of Dark Grey with White fuselage top decking. The aircraft were operated in the ASW role armed with A244 lightweight torpedoes. (J.Visanich)

This C-47, of the South Arabian Air Force during November of 1967, was based at Khormaksar, Aden.

Algeria was one of several Arab air forces to operate the early Mi-24 Hind A gunship. Libya also flew the Hind A.

This overall Natural Metal Vampire FB.52 (serial L282) was flown by the Lebanese Air Force from Kleyate during 1954.

This Sudanese Air Force Provost T.53 carries the insignia used by Sudan prior to 1983. Sudan flew the Provost during the late 1950s and early 1960s.

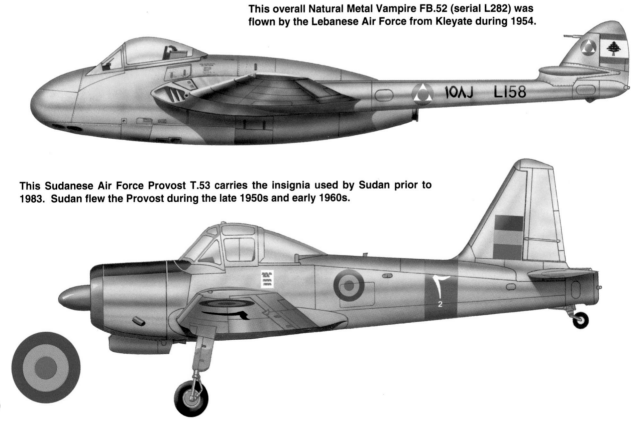

This Libyan Army Agusta-Bell AB-206A JetRanger (serialed 8185) was donated to the Armed Forces of Malta in June 1973. The aircraft had just arrived in Marla on its delivery flight and still carried Libyan pre-1977 roundels. In Maltese service, the aircraft was registered 9H-AAJ. (J. Visanich)

Rising oil prices substantially multiplied Libya's foreign income. In an arms-for-oil agreement with France, thirty-eight Mirage F.1AD/F.1ED/F.1BD fighters were ordered during 1974. The LARAF purchased a variety of helicopters, including twenty Meridionali-built CH-47C Chinooks and a single Agusta-built Sikorsky AS.61A VIP machine from Italy. Ten ex-Italian Army Cessna 0-1 Bird Dogs were received by the Libyan Army which eventually also operated the Chinooks.

Soviet Influence

The Soviet Union's courting of Libya had started in 1970 when quantities of army equipment was supplied. Soviet naval base facilities in Libyan ports were, however, refused. During 1974, a bilateral agreement provided for the training of Libyan aircrews in the USSR and in Libya as well as the construction of a SAM air defense system for Libyan airfields was concluded. In return, Gaddafi conceded to allow V-VS aircraft to use Libyan air bases, the first Tu-22 bombers being sighted at Okba bin Nafi in 1974. That same year the LARAF ordered some fifty MiG-23BN strike fighters and a small number of MiG-15UTI trainers while fifty SOKO G-2A Galebs were purchased from Yugoslavia for the eventual replacement of the Magisters. In March of 1974, the Air Academy was established at Zawia, this school being instrumental in greatly increasing the number of indigenous pilots, although the fast influx of modern weaponry for the LARAF necessitated the recruitment of an ever-increasing number of foreign crews.

By the end of 1975, the LARAF was composed of four interceptor squadrons, two equipped with thirty-two Mirage 5Ds and the others with MiG-23 Flogger Es; four ground attack squadrons with fifty Mirage 5DEs, one reconnaissance unit flying ten Mirage 5DRs; two transport units were equipped with eight C-130Hs and nine C-47s while a number of helicopter units were formed flying various types, including twelve Mi-8s, ten Alouette IIIs, nine Super Frelons, two AB-206s and the first

Both the Libyan Army and Libyan Air Force operate Alouette III helicopters on liaison and training duties. The army procured a total of thirteen which appeared in at least two color schemes, the camouflaged version being painted in a Green/Tan/Purple-Gray scheme with Light Blue undersurfaces and a roundel carried on the cabin sides. (J. Visanich)

The first eight of a Libyan order for sixteen C-130H Hercules transports were delivered by early 1971, but in 1973 the U.S. imposed an embargo on deliveries. Many of the C-130s in LARAF service were left in their original White over Natural Metal, like 113, which still carried the early LARAF Red/White/Black roundels. (G. Mangion)

A number of C-130Hs of the LARAF, like 115, were camouflaged in Dark Earth and Sand uppersurfaces over Azure Blue undersurfaces. The Green disc roundel carried on LARAF aircraft came into use during 1977. Libyan C-130s are grouped in one unit at Benina Air Base and have participated in many of Colonel Gaddafi's adventures in Africa, including Uganda in 1972 and 1979 where at least one, 116, was shot down, and in Chad during the 1980s. (Author)

of the Chinooks, most of these actually belonging to the fledgling army aviation organization. Trainers were stationed at the Air Academy but the two-seat variants of the MiG-23s and Mirages remained with their respective units as conversion trainers. Training facilities were enhanced during the mid-1970s when no less than 230 SIAI SF-260WL Warriors were ordered for the Zawia Academy and for government sponsored aero-clubs around the country. By 1979, up to 5,000 Soviet military

Another scheme carried by Libyan Alouette IIIs was this Azure Blue and White, with a Gray-outlined badge on the cabin and the roundel, the post-1977 Green disc, on the horizontal and vertical stabilizers. Three Alouette IIIs were donated to the Armed Forces of Malta, including this aircraft, serial 2295. (J. Visanich)

41

In 1973, twenty Meridionali-built CH-47C Chinooks were sold to Libya by Italy. Serialed LC-001 to 020, the Chinooks were operated by the Libyan Army in a Dark Earth/Sand camouflage with Light Blue undersurfaces. The serial was carried on the rear rotor housing below the Arabic characters, and was repeated on the lower fuselage forward of the Green disc national marking. (Author)

advisors were reported to be in Libya, in addition to North Koreans, Pakistanis, Palestinians, Czechs, East Germans, Cubans as well as French, Yugoslavs and Taiwanese. It was estimated that by 1979 there were only 150 Libyan pilots qualified to fly the 260 LARAF combat aircraft. This is a very low pilot to aircraft ratio, when compared to the usual normal ratio in western air forces of two pilots per aircraft.

By then the Soviets were firmly established in Libya and their influence was extended to the organizational set-up of the LARAF in which the Air Regiment became the basic unit, normally composed of three squadrons of twelve aircraft each performing broadly the same role. V-VS MiG-25Rs were operating from Okba bin Nafi on reconnaissance flights over the U.S. Sixth Fleet and Tu-22s in Libyan markings were spotted over the Mediterranean during 1977. Twelve Tu-22s had, in fact, entered service with the LARAF, with a second unit forming with the TU-22 during 1980.

On the other hand, relations with Egypt were worsening and in July of 1977, Libyan artillery attacked Egypt across the border as a sign of discord over Egypt's peace initiative with Israel. In reply, Egyptian Su-20s and MiG-21s attacked Libyan radar sites and villages, bombed the Mirage base at Nasser Air Base and struck at Al Kurta airfield. On the other hand, LARAF aircraft, particularly Mirage 5s, bombed Egyptian border villages during which one Mirage was claimed to have been shot

The LARAF operated up to eighteen Antonov An-26 Curl medium transports and ten are thought to be still in service. Serialed in the 8300 range (except for two which were observed with serials in the 3800 range) the An-26s were involved in Libya's war in Chad, at least two having been destroyed in Chad. Their entry into Libyan service enabled the C-47s to be relegated to navigational training role. (J.Visanich)

Interest in the Italian Aeritalia G.222 transport met with U.S. refusal to sanction the sale of the GE T64 engines powering the aircraft, but Aeritalia offered to re-engine a prototype with Rolls-Royce Tyne turboprops. The aircraft met Libyan requirements and some twenty G.222Ts were delivered to the LARAF (serialed 221 to 240). (Author)

Delivered in Czech civil markings but carrying full Libyan camouflage, a number of LET L-410T Turbolets were delivered to the LARAF between March of 1983 and February of 1986. These aircraft OK-NZA, -NZB and -NZC were delivered on 30 January 1984. In Libyan service they operated in training and paramilitary roles. (J.Visanich)

down by a SAM. During this brief four day war, during which half a dozen aircraft on each side were lost, Libyan Mi-8 Hip J helicopters, allegedly Soviet-crewed, carried out radar-jamming operations against Egyptian defenses.

By the late 1970s, Libya was earning for itself notoriety by its interference in the internal affairs of other African countries and by its association with such infamous figures as Idi Amin of Uganda and Emperor Bokassa of the Central African Empire.

The War in Chad

Petro-dollars enabled the LARAF to expand and after the delivery of the thirty-eight Mirage F.1s during 1979/80, a further twenty-six F.1EDs

Increasing income from rising oil prices during the mid-1970s enabled Libya to buy the best. In 1974, thirty-eight Mirage F.1 fighters were ordered from France, including sixteen F.1ED multi-role fighters. (AMD-BA)

Libyan Sukhoi Su-20/22 Fitters were often met in the air by U.S.Navy fighters. This machine, an Su-22 Fitter F is fully armed with AA-2 Atoll air-to-air missiles, long range fuel tanks and with what appear to be AA-8 Aphid short range dog-fight air-to-air missiles on the forward pylons. The chin-mounted laser target seeker is very conspicuous. Libya lost two Fitters in an encounter with F-14s during March of 1976. The Libyan flight leader had opened fire on the F-14s with an AA-2 missiles and the F-14s responded with AIM-9 Sidewinders, shooting down both Fitters. (USN)

were ordered, while supplies of MiG-23 Flogger E interceptors had reached 143 in 1981 in addition to a number of Flogger F close-support aircraft. During 1981, the first confirmation was received that the LARAF was using Su-22 Fitter J attack aircraft, thirty-six being based at Okba bin Nafi, 100 being reportedly in use by 1982. Close to sixty MiG-25 Foxbat-A/Bs were also in service, while in 1984, Libya became the only foreign operator of the advanced Foxbat D reconnaissance and ELINT aircraft. Ilyushin Il-76Ms and Il-76TDs were used alternately by the LARAF and the national airline, while twenty Aeritalia G.222T transports, powered by Rolls Royce Tyne engines, entered service.

Libya's involvement in the civil war in Chad was a major episode in LARAF history. The service was very active in Chad, using Mirage F.1s and Tu-22s in 1981. The lack of proper airfields in southern Libya hindered operations and extensive use was later made of SF-260WL Warriors in the light strike role, while Chinooks and Hercules transports were employed to transport several thousand Libyan troops and army material into the war zone. As the war dragged on, LARAF activity was very much in evidence, MiG-23s being also used in the later stages. During 1987, the opposing forces advanced northwards, even invading Libyan territory and capturing large quantities of Libyan army equipment and a number of aircraft. Total LARAF losses in the air or captured in this war amounted to two Tu-22s, two MiG-23s, one MiG-25, two An-26s, seventeen SF-260s, fifteen L-39Z0s, eleven Mi-24s and six SA-13 SAM batteries.

Libyan-US Confrontations

As Gaddafi expanded his international involvement he was apt to come into confrontation with Western interests, particularly the U.S. In March and September of 1973 LARAF Mirage 5s had opened fire on a USAF EC-130 and a RC-135 respectively which were on ELINT duties in the Gulf of Sirte, compelling Libya to declare the whole Gulf as national waters, contrary to international practice.

On 19 August 1981, during Sixth Fleet exercises, a USN E-2C Hawkeye picked two LARAF aircraft approaching the U.S. carrier group and two F-14 Tomcats were vectored to the target. At close range

The Libyan Air Force acquired a number of Tu-22 Blinder supersonic bombers, of which seven are still thought to be in service. These aircraft were often encountered by U.S. Navy aircraft over the international waters. (USN)

By 1978 the LARAF became a favored customer for the MiG-25 Foxbat Mach 3 fighter and after two years some sixty Foxbat As and Foxbat Bs were in service, while in 1982 Libya became the only, foreign operator of the advanced Foxbat D ELINT version. This Foxbat E is a converted Foxbat A with upgraded radar and limited look down/shoot down capability. It is carrying AA-6 Acrid missiles on the inboard pylon and a pair of AA-8 short range missiles on the outboard pylons. (USN)

The MiG-23 Flogger has been in the Libyan inventory since 1975 when some fifty Flogger E air defense variants were delivered. Larger deliveries were later to be received, including the Flogger F close support variants and Flogger G air defense varaints. These Flogger Gs were intercepted over the Mediterranean during 1980 by U.S. Navy fighters. They are armed with AA-2 Atoll air-to-air missiles on both the fuselage and underwing pylons. A pair of Floggers were shot down by U.S. Navy F-14A Tomcats over the Gulf of Sirte on 4 January 1989. (USN)

Eight Aerospatiale Rallye Club light planes were purchased for the Libyan Air Force in 1982, four each of the 180E and 235GT models. This 180E variant, still carries its French delivery registration, but with full LARAF insignia. The Rallye Clubs were used by the LARAF for primary training. (J. Visanich)

the LARAF leader fired an AA-2 Atoll AAM, which missed the F-14s. They responded, firing two AIM-9L Sidewinders at the Libyan aircraft, later identified as Su-22 Fitter Js and shooting down both intruders.

In March of 1986, Libyan shore batteries of SA-2s and SA-5s fired at USN aircraft taking part in an exercise in the Gulf of Sirte. The U.S. retaliated, sinking a Libyan missile patrol boat and a corvette and attacking the SAM sites with A-6 Intruders and A-7 Corsairs. The matter seemed to have ended there but the explosion of a bomb on 5 April in a West Berlin discotheque, which killed an American serviceman and injured several others, was blamed on Libya. In Operation EL DORADO CANYON (15 April), the U.S. hit back. UK-based F-111Fs attacked a terrorist camp at Murrat Sidi Bilal, the Azzizziyah barracks and the military side of Tripoli International Airport, while USN A-6Es from the carriers USS CORAL SEA and AMERICA attacked the Al Jamahiriya barracks near Benghazi and Benina Air Base. The attack achieved total surprise and was over so quickly that no LARAF aircraft were able to intercept. One F-111F was lost during the raids but several LARAF aircraft were destroyed on the ground including six Il-76s, one G.222, four MiG23s, two Mi-8s as well as two F.27 Friendships and a Boeing 727 civil aircraft. The raid had accomplished its political aim of subduing Gaddafi into easing his support for international terrorism.

Libyan and USN fighters were again in action during 1989 over the disputed Gulf of Sirte. On 4 January, two F-14As from the USS JOHN F. KENNEDY on a CAP station over their carrier group, were warned by an E-2C that two unidentified aircraft, later confirmed as Libyan MiG-23 Floggers, were on a course towards the carrier and about eighty-two miles distant. After effecting a number of course changes which the Libyans insisted on following, the Navy pilots decided that the Floggers posed a threat to their carrier and launched two AIM-7 Sparrow AAMs which missed. At a range of five miles, the Tomcats fired another Sparrow and a Sidewinder, both missiles hitting their targets and downing both Floggers.

The LAJAF

The war in Chad had elicited a French embargo on arms supplies to Libya which lasted until 1989. In the meantime, Libya had searched for other sources of supply and thirty SOKO Jastrebs were purchased from Yugoslavia for the light strike role. Supplies from the USSR remained no problem. By 1988, the air force changed its name to Libyan Arab Jamahiriya Air Force (LAJAF), and it was estimated that seven Tu-22s, sixty MiG-25s,130 MiG-23s, eighty Su-22s, fifty MiG-21s, thirty-five Mirage Fls and seventy-five Mirage 5s remained in service. It appears that earlier Libyan requests for newer Soviet equipment such as MiG-29 Fulcrums and Su-24 Fencers were refused. During 1989, a reversal of this Soviet decision led to the delivery of six Fencer Ds, Libya becoming the first foreign operator of the Fencer.

The use of the MiG-21 in Libyan service has always raised questions and some agencies insist that the aircraft were actually in Libya for the use of PLO air crews, although this was never confirmed.

Relations between Libya and the Western world remain tense, particularly after Libyan terrorists were blamed for causing the loss of a Pan Am 747 over Lockerbie, Scotland during December of 1988 and a UTA airliner over Niger in September of 1989. An international embargo was imposed and remains in effect, but military action of the type taken against Iraq in 1990 is discouraged by other Arab states who have already signified their disinvolvement. The embargo has paralyzed the LAJAF now that the former major source of supply, the USSR, no longer exists, although North Korea is believed to be supplying a limited amount of arms.

Grounding of LAJAF aircraft for lack of spares is widespread and the future of the force is, at present, unknown.

Mauritania

Force Airienne Isiamlque de Mauritanie (Islamic Air Force of Mauritania)

Mauritania gained independence from France in November of 1960, and formed an air element, the Groupement Aerienne de 1a Republique Islamique de Mauritanie, with one C-47 and two Max Holste MN-1521M Broussard light transports donated by the French government. These aircraft were operated from the main airfield at Nouakchott, which also served as the International Airport.

For several years, transport and liaison remained the main roles for the air element which was soon given air force status and renamed Force Aerienne Islamique de Mauritanie (FAIM). For the most part, its aircraft were flown by seconded French Air Force pilots but training of local pilots began when six MS.881 Rallye trainers were procured during 1970. Reflecting its main transport role, particularly linking Nouakchott, the capital, with several desert air strips, the FAIM sought to increase the C-47 fleet and in 1966, the inventory was increased to six while an additional three Broussards were also obtained, all being surplus French equipment.

The C-47s were formed into an Escadrille de Transport while the Broussards were grouped into an Escadrille de Liaison, the latter being strengthened in 1971/73 by seven ex-Niger Air Force Cessna-Reims F-337 Skymasters and second-hand Aermacchi AL.60Bs. In 1974, two Douglas C-54s were acquired to supplement the Dakotas in the transport unit. In November of the following year, the first new aircraft for the FAIM, two Short Skyvan 3Ms, joined the transport unit. The British aircraft's short, rough-field take-off capability was greatly appreciated and it became an essential part of the inventory. A Caravelle 6R jet trans-

Purchased to modernize its military training fleet, twelve Beech T-34C-1 Turbo-Mentors joined the Moroccan Air Force during 1977. Morocco was the first export customer for the T-34C. The Turbo-Mentors are based at the Base Ecole des Forces Royales Air at Marrakech. Before the introduction of modern types as the T-34C-1, a substantial portion of the training syllabus had been undertaken in France. (Beech)

An Omani Beaver AL.1 (XR214) taking off from Firq, one of a hundred dust strips constructed all over the country to facilitate communications and the transport of troops. This air transport capability became decisive in crushing the insurgency. (RAF)

With air defense taken care of, the FARM could concentrate on its war with the Polisario. Six ex-USMC OV-10A Broncos, twenty-five F-5E/Fs, twenty-four SA.342L Gazelles, and six Meridionali-built CH-47C Chinooks were all on order or delivered by 1979.

These relatively large acquisitions, together with the war with Polisario, were draining the Moroccan economy. By 1980, Polisario SAMs had claimed four Mirages, two helicopters and several F-5s, as well as damaging a C-130. The army commitment had increased from 50,000 in 1976 to 116,000 in 1981. These troops manned a 312-mile long defensive line constructed to prevent Polisario infiltration. Mirages, including the new F.lEHs at Sidi Slimane, were fitted with chaff/flare dispensers to defeat the SAM threat.

In 1979, seven ex-USAF F-5Es were transferred to the FARM to make up for losses, but the escalating cost of the war and the normalization of relations with Algeria during 1988 helped bring the conflict to an end. A formal cease-fire did not go into effect until September of 1991 and even then, spasmodic fighting along the front still went on.

The last of the Mirage F.lEHs were delivered in 1984, but Morocco did not take up its option for another twenty-five. In 1985, interest was shown in both the Mirage 2000 and the Northrop F-20A Tiger Shark as a possible replacement for both the Mirage F.1s and the F-5, but no further progress was made due to economic constraints.

Twenty USAF F-16As/Bs were ordered in 1991, while the remaining forty Mirage F.Is were recently refurbished by Dassault. The Mirage 2000 order is being reconsidered, thirty-five examples being possibly financed by the UAE. Efforts to enhance the transport fleet resulted in seven Airtec CN-235Ms being purchased in 1989, thanks to a Spanish long-term loan.

Although a small but compact and balanced force with fairly modern equipment and a sound training base, the FARM will have to make a decision on the acquisition of a first-line modern combat aircraft to supplement and ultimately replace its present first-line types in the near future.

A waiting Arab sits in the shade of an Omani Short Skyvan 3m (serial 902). The climate and the dusty airfields of Oman in the 1970s presented probably the most punishing conditions for any aircraft to operated in. Even in the shade, temperatures often reached 123 degrees (F), 51 degrees Celsius. (G. J.Kamp)

Six Short Skyvan 3Ms were ordered by the Omani Air Force in May of 1970, the first arriving at Bait al Falej on 2 June. In all, the SOAF operated sixteen Skyvans, all delivered between 1970 and 1975. At least two have crashed (905 and 909). Seven were fitted with a Racal surveillance radar and used for SAR and maritime patrol duties. (G. J. Kamp)

Oman

Al quwwat al jawwiya al Malakiya Oman (Royal Air Force of Oman)

Relations between Britain and Oman date back to 1798, when the British, aware of this important trade route post in the Strait of Hormuz, assisted the local sultan to suppress rival tribesmen.

The Sultan of Oman turned to Britain for assistance again in 1957 when a rebellion threatened his throne. British forces quelled the uprising but also persuaded the feudal and conservative ruler to create an air force. As a result, on 1 March 1959, the Sultan of Oman Air Force (SOAF) became operational with two Scottish Aviation Pioneer CC.1. These were soon followed by three Hunting Provost T.52 trainers, which had strengthened wings to carry twenty-five pound bombs, 0.303 inch Browning machine gun pods or two inch rockets. This miniature force, paid for and staffed by Britain, was initially under the command of Squadron Leader G. B. Atkinson, RAF. The non-existence of an educational base for native Omanis precluded the recruitment of locals and the SOAF became a rather mercenary force, dependent on foreigners (mostly British) to fly and maintain its aircraft. Thirty years later this situation has been much improved, although a totally Omani run air force will take several more years to achieve as more sophisticated equipment enters service.

In 1960, two more Provosts, another Pioneer and four DHC Beavers entered service. These played a limited role in operations against rebel forces, mostly facilitating communications with far-flung settlements

During 1970, the DHC-4 Caribou was selected by the SOAF as a successor to the aging C-47 transports. Three were initially ordered, this number being eventually increased to five (serials 801-805). Together with the Short Skyvan, the Caribou became the only link, apart from donkey and camel, with the remote, far-flung outposts all around Oman. (Author)

In 1970, four AB-206A Jet Rangers were introduced to form a helicopter element for the Omani Air Force. The rugged topography of the country was suited to helicopter operations, since helicopters could reach areas which had virtually remained untouched by modern civilization. The Omani Air Force went on to purchase three Bell-built Jet Rangers. (G. J.Kamp)

Four Westland Wessex HC.2 helicopters were loaned to the SOAF by the RAF, apparently repainted in a camouflage scheme of Dark Earth/Light Stone with Black undersurfaces. While in SOAF service, the Wessexes retained their RAF serials. (G. J. Kamp)

A No. 4 Squadron BAC-111 of the Air Force of the Sultanate of Oman, still carrying the original serial 1002. The aircraft was later renumbered 502. (G.J.Kamp)

In the early 1970s, a number of Vickers Viscount airliners were purchased by the Sultan of Oman Air Force. Serialed 505, this Viscount Series 808 was an ex-Aer Lingus aircraft and entered Omani service in April of 1973. These aircraft carried the last digit of serial number, 5, on fin. This machine was withdrawn from use in September of 1976. (M. Pace)

In 1974/75, three BAC 111 Series 485 jet transports were procured by the SOAF for passenger, troop transport and freight services. Serialed 1001-1003 (later changed to 550-553), the BAC 111s of No 4 Squadron provided a nation-wide scheduled free passenger service for Omanis. (M. Pace)

and providing a base for the training of local Omanis in aircraft flying and maintenance. Close to a hundred air strips were constructed in the desert, enabling the fast movement of troops anywhere in Oman from the main SOAF base at Bait al Falej.

During 1962, more serious trouble arose in the southern Dhofar region when rebels, backed by Egypt and Iraq, opposed the Sultan's dictatorial rule. Operating from the rugged hills and mountains, the Sultan's troops found difficulty in suppressing this new movement, a situation exacerbated when Britain relinquished its base in nearby Aden during 1967. The SOAF's Provosts could hardly oppose the new ground-to-air weapons being obtained by the Dhofaris from China and an order for twelve BAC Strikemaster Mk.82 was placed with Britain. Delivered in 1969, these soon showed their capability to attack rebel strongholds, but the conservative Sultan was loath to expand his armed forces in spite of increasing oil revenues. A successful palace coup carried out by his son, Qaboos, in July of 1970 opened a new era for the SOAF.

Orders were placed for Short Skyvan 3M and DHC-4 Caribous to replace the old C-47s obtained in 1968. The Strikemaster order was increased to twenty-four, while a number of Vickers Viscount airliners were purchased to serve as troop transports. A helicopter unit was created and in a few years grew to include four AB-206s, eight AB-205s and two AB-212s with five Bell 214s being operated by the Omani Police. Saudi Arabia donated army equipment while two squadrons of Bell 205s, complete with crews, were donated by Iran, in exchange for Iranian ownership of Goat Island in the Strait of Hormuz. During 1974, three BAC 111s, eight BN.2 Defenders and a Vickers VC-10 were purchased, but the real turning point came later that year when thirty-one Hawker Hunters were donated to the SOAF by Jordan, while an order for twelve SEPECAT Jaguar International strike aircraft was placed with England for delivery during 1977/78. Facilities at Salalah, Masirah

48

This Omani Hawker Hunter FR.73 of No 6 Squadron carries low visibility national markings on the fin. The aircraft was camouflaged in an overall Gray. (USN via Nicholas J. Waters III)

Omani Jaguars were flown by BAC pilots from Warton, England via Toulouse, France and Malta, on their way to the Middle East. Aircraft 203, a two-seat Jaguar International B, was delivered on 27-28 June 1977, and was assigned to No 8 Squadron at Thumrait. (Author)

Island, Bait al Falej and various desert strips were improved for jet aircraft operations while a new runway was constructed at Midway (renamed Thumrait).

Operations by Hunters (flown by British and Jordanian pilots), Strikemasters and Defenders, some even inside South Yemen, were instrumental in breaking the Dhofari rebels and by December of 1975, the insurgency was declared ended.

This Omani Jaguar was conducting joint exercises with the U.S. Navy on 17 December 1979 and was carrying a practice bomb carrier on the centerline stores station. The aircraft was flown by a British contract officer. (USN via Nicholas J. Waters III)

Nos 8 and 20 Squadrons operated a total of twenty-six SEPECAT Jaguars. All carried a wrap-round camouflage of Dark Earth/Light Stone. The Jaguars, although primarily strike aircraft, had a secondary air defence role. (J. Visanich)

With the service entry of the Jaguar during 1977, the Strikemasters of No 1 Squadron at Salalah were relegated to armament training with a secondary strike role, while No 6 Squadron's Hunters at Thumrait continued in the ground-attack role, although in later years they were fitted

Patrolling over typically rugged Omani terrain, this pair of Jaguar Internationals are from the second batch, delivered during 1983. These differed from the aircraft of the first batch in a number of respects, including the provision to carry overwing Matra 550 Magic air-to-air missiles in addition to the usual underwing AIM-9P Sidewinders. (BAe)

Qatar intended to purchase twelve Hunters during 1971, but financial problems caused a reduction of deliveries to three Hunter F.78s and one T. 79, all being ex-Royal Netherlands Air Force aircraft. The Hunters served a total of some ten years in the Qatar Emiri Air Force. (Author)

with AIM-9 Sidewinders for a secondary air defense role. The Jaguars equipped No 8 Squadron at Thumrait (later moving to Masirah) and a repeat order for a second batch of twelve, delivered in 1983, formed No 20 Squadron at Masirah Island. This second batch were configured for Matra AAMs on over-wing mounts.

Enhancement of the transport fleet, so essential in a country with poor land communications, was made in 1981 with the delivery of the first of three C-130H Hercules transports, while the Skyvans, later fitted with a Racal surveillance radar, and the Defenders carried out maritime patrol and SAR work. The six surviving BN Defenders were disposed of during 1993.

During 1985, Oman placed an order for eight Tornado ADVs, although this was later changed to eight Hawk 103s and eight Hawk 203s when oil revenues began to fall off. The Hawks were delivered during 1993/94 replacing the aging Hunters which were finally retired in November of 1993. During 1990, the air force changed its designation from SOAF to Royal Air Force of Oman (RAFO).

The Royal Flight operates a variety of aircraft, including a Boeing 747SP, a DC-8-73, two Gulfstream IIs and two AS.332 Super Pumas.

Qatar
Qatar Emiri Air Force

Until 1971, Qatar, a peninsula in the Persian Gulf, was, in effect, a British Protectorate ruled by an Emir. Imminent British withdrawal from the Gulf necessitated the setting up of a local defense force and on 30 March 1968, a Public Security Force was formed. This force included an Air Wing, which was established with British assistance. The Air Wing was initially equipped with two Westland Whirlwind Series 3 helicopters operated by seconded RAF personnel.

The following year interest was shown in introducing a combat element and, in 1971, an order for three refurbished Hunter F.78s and one T.79 trainer, was placed, with delivery taking place during December of that year.

For some years, these remained the sole equipment of the air arm which, in 1974, was made independent from the Public Security Forces and renamed Qatar Emiri Air Force (QEAF), although its role remained that of supporting the land forces. To strengthen this mission, four Westland Commando Mk.2A assault helicopters were ordered to form No 9 Transport Squadron, one machine being fitted as a VIP Mk.2C, enabling the retirement of the Whirlwinds. In the meantime, the Qatar Police, a separate corps, received two Westland-built SA.341G Gazelles which the force operated until the machines were incorporated into the QEAF's inventory in 1983.

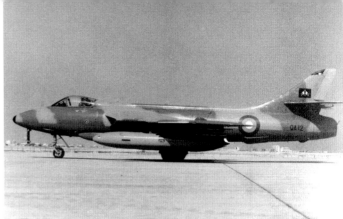

This Hunter F.78 (QA 11) of the Qatar EAF was delivered on 20 December 1971, in company with another Hunter (QA 10). For most of their careers in the QEAF, the Hunters were flown by ex-RAF contract pilots. (M. Pace)

The fin flash insignia carried on this Hunter F.78 (QA 12) was a replica of the Qatar national flag. The crossed flags are Red and White on a Black background with the shield between the flags in Gold. (Author)

Increasing oil revenues enabled Qatar to improve its military equipment and in December of 1979 the QEAF placed an order for six Alpha Jet 1Es. The first three arrived at Doha Air Base, the only airfield in

Six delivery positions vacated by the Ivory Coast Air Force, which cancelled six from its order for Alpha Jets enabled Qatar to start receiving its allotment of six aircraft in October of 1980. Serialed QA 50 to QA 55, the Qatar Alpha Jet 1Es equip No 11 Close Support Squadron at Doha, replacing the Hawker Hunters. In addition, the Alpha Jets are also used in the weapons training role. (Author)

Qatar's Westland Commando Mk.2s have uprated Gnome tur-boshafts and sand filters for operating in a typical Middle East environ-ment. Four Mk.2As were ordered in 1974 for the assault role, but one was outfitted as a VIP Mk.2C. In 1981, eight Commando Mk.8s were ordered for the anti-shipping role. (Author)

The Qatar Emiri Air Force took delivery of twelve Mirage F.1EDA fighters and two F.1DDA trainers in March of 1983. They were ini-tially retained in France for the training of Qatari personnel and their actual arrival at Doha did not take place before July of 1984. Qatari Mirages, operated by No 7 Squadron, are multi-role variants and can carry cameras and Matra 550 Magic air-to-air missiles. Two are kept on alert status round-the-clock to intercept any intruders into Qatari airspace. (Author)

Qatar, during October of 1980, followed by the next batch. These air-craft formed No 11 Close Support Squadron. In late 1980, an order was placed with France for twelve Mirage F.1EDAs and two F.1DDA train-ers. The Mirage's were optimized for air defense and the contract also included pilot training in France. In fact, the first aircraft did not reach Qatar before July of 1984, having been retained at Mont-de-Marsan and in Orange for use by the Qatari trainees. At Doha, the Mirages formed No 7 Air Superiority Squadron.

The rotary wing fleet was given importance during the 1980s. Six AS.330F Super Pumas were received in 1982 to supplement No 9

As part of a large U.K. order, Saudi Arabia received four Hunter F.60 fighters and two T.66 trainers. All were delivered to No 6 Squadron at Khamis Mushayt in May of 1966. This aircraft (serial 601) was in transit at Luqa, Malta. It had previously been XJ712, an F.6 of the RAF, before being rebuilt for Saudi Arabia. (Bob Elliot)

Squadron's Commando Mk.2s while eight Commando Mk.3s and twelve HOT-armed SA.342L Gazelles were purchased in 1983. The Commandos were formed into No 8 Anti-Surface Vessel Squadron, with two of the helicopters being fitted to carry one AM.39 Exocet. The Gazelles equipped No 6 Close Support Squadron which also absorbed the Qatari Police's two SA.341G Gazelles and three Westland Lynx Mk.28s for liaison and observation duties. Other aircraft procured during this period were two Boeing 707s and a Boeing 727 for use by govern-ment high officials.

From 1980 on, the Gulf was an uneasy area due to the Iran-Iraq War, which ended in 1988. This was soon followed in August of 1990 by Iraq's invasion of nearby Kuwait. Feeling threatened, Qatar requested Western assistance and USAF, Canadian and French strike aircraft were soon at Doha alongside the QEAF's own combat aircraft.

The QEAF's Mirages and Alpha Jets took an active part in Operation DESERT STORM, undertaking escort missions for Coalition strike air-craft on raids into occupied Kuwait and southern Iraq. It was the first time the QEAF went into action and the experience proved that this modest force would be prepared for combat should Qatar's sovereignty be endangered.

During mid-1994, it was reported that Qatar's eleven surviving Mirage F.1EDAs and two F.1DDAs were sold to the Spanish Air Force.

Saudi Arabia

Al Quwwat al Jawwiya Al Malakiya as Sa'udiya (Royal Saudi Air Force)

Perhaps representing the major constant factor in an Arab world of shifting alliances, Saudi Arabia has remained staunchly pro-Western since the Kingdom's foundation by King Ibn Saud during 1931. Even before that, the King, then just the Sultan of Neid, had encouraged the formation of a small air arm. During 1923, this force, known as the Al Saud Air Arm, was made up of ex-RAF deHavilland DH-9 bombers, which were later joined by four ex-RAF Westland Wapitis. British pilots and technicians were engaged to operate and maintain the aircraft at Dhahran airfield with the maintenance workshops being located at Jedda. Jedda was later expanded to include an airfield. Italian engineers were offered by the Fascist government of Italy to take over the con-struction of Jedda during 1937, after the Saudi-British cooperation agreement had expired.

The Second World War postponed further development; in fact the air All Saudi Hunters were camouflaged in a Dark Earth, Light Stone uppersurface camouflage with Azure Blue undersurfaces. The leg-end on the fuselage was in Green. In early 1967, Saudi Hunters (except for one which had crashed) were presented to the Jordanian Air Force. (Bob Elliot)

This Saudi Strikemaster Mk.80, serial 903, passed through Malta during its transit in 1968. It was accompanied by a second Strikemaster, number 904, also in the overall Gray scheme. The first two Strikemasters delivered to Saudi Arabia, 901 and 902, had been delivered in a camouflage pattern. 903 was written off in a crash on 8 December 1970. (G. Mangion)

(Right) Not all Saudi Strikemasters were delivered in a camouflage finish. Some, like 903, were finished in overall Light Aircraft Grey. Otherwise, the aircraft carried the same markings as the camouflaged Strikemasters, except that the rear fuselage logos were painted in Green directly onto the Gray fuselage. (Author)

This Dark Earth and Sand over Azure Blue camouflaged Saudi Strikemaster Mk.80 (serial 1111) was in transit through Malta during July of 1969. It was accompanied by two other aircraft, numbers 1112 and 1113. (Author)

The serial numbers of Royal Saudi Air Force Strikemasters was repeated in both English and Arabic on the nose and tail. The anti-glare panel on the nose was in Flat Black. (Author)

DHC Chipmunk T.10s obtained from Britain became, in 1956, the standard primary trainer of the Royal Saudi Air Force. Based at Taif the Chipmunks gave invaluable service by providing a pool of trained pilots in the early years of the air force. (Author)

arm, which had been renamed the Royal Hijazi Air Force during 1925 and Royal Saudi Arabian Air Force in 1931, apparently ceased to exist, but the visit of a British military mission in 1950 and the country's increased oil wealth enabled the present Royal Saudi Air Force (RSAF) to be established. A number of ex-RAF DH Tiger Moth and Auster Aiglet trainers, and Avro Anson light transports were acquired while U.S. MDAP funds (following a U.S.-Saudi base agreement for Dhahran) brought ten Temco TE-1A Buckaroos and T-6 Texan trainers, along with C-47 transports and pilot training. Such training was also undertaken with British private firms and in Egypt, but the first combat aircraft for the new RSAF came from the U.S. during 1955 in the form of three B-26B Invaders, followed by an additional six the following year. Training was given an impetus with the acquisition in 1956 of twelve DHC Chipmunk T.10s and five Beech T-34 Mentors in 1957 while Egypt donated four DH Vampire FB.52s in 1957, with additional Vampires being supplied later. The Vampire becoming the RSAF's first jet equipment.

With the extension of the Dhahran base agreement in 1957, six Fairchild C-123B transports were added to the inventory. Besides Dhahran and Jedda, airfields had been constructed at Taif, Medina, Khamis Mushayt, Yanbu and Jubail for the use of the RSAF, while the

The Royal Saudi Air Force logo on the rear fuselage was painted in Green against a White panel in both English and Arabic. The serial was in Black against the camouflage, again in both English and Arabic. (Author)

The Royal Flight of Saudi Arabia had one Lockheed Jetstar and the air force operated two as VIP transports. This Jetstar was the aircraft assigned to the air force. Serialed 103 (the other Jetstar carried the serial 102), it remained in service with the RSAF from 1969 to 1986, flying with No 1 Squadron at Riyadh. (J. Visanich)

Apart from Kuwait, Saudi Arabia was the only export customer of the BAC Lightning. Eighteen Lightning F.53s and four Lightning T.55s were purchased, but they saw little actual service before they were replaced by the F-15 Eagle. (BAC)

Like the Jordanian Air Force, the RSAF uses serials that relate to units. This C-130H (serial 1615) belongs to No 16 Squadron. It was delivered in July of 1977 and was one of fifty-five C-130s purchased by the RSAF. (S. Bottaro)

Losing out to the BAC Lightning F.53 in a 1965 Saudi competition, the F-5E was later ordered for the Royal Saudi Air Force in the 1970s. Some seventy being delivered. The RSAF also operated ten RF-5Es, twenty-four F-5Fs and twenty F-5Bs. F-5Es are still in service with Nos 3, 10, 15 and 17 Squadrons. No 17 Squadron also operates the RF-5E reconnaissance fighter. (Northrop)

airfield of Riyadh doubled as a civil airport. The U.S. had invested well in Saudi Arabia and twelve F-86F Sabre jet fighters and ten Lockheed T-33A jet trainers (all ex-USAF) were transferred through MAP during 1957/58, the former replacing the Vampires of No 5 Squadron.

The situation, however, was better on paper than in reality. The Invaders were grounded most of the time for lack of spares, while the Sabres were delivered without their usual six gun armament. Shortages of pilots was another problem which required years to solve. A sharp reminder of the RSAF's immobility came in 1962 when civil war erupted in neighboring Yemen between republicans, backed by Egypt, and royalists, which Saudi Arabia supported. Several jet combat units of the Egyptian Air Force were deployed to Yemen and frequently struck Saudi territory, the RSAF finding itself powerless to hit back. An air defense system supported by fast.jet interceptors was required and the British Aircraft Corporation (BAC) won the contract, known as "Magic Carpet" during 1965 against fierce competition from the U.S. and France. The contract called for the immediate delivery from RAF stocks of four Lightning F.52s, two Lightning T.54 trainers, four Hunter F.60s and two Hunter T.70 trainers, in addition to ex-British Army Thunderbird SAM batteries. Khamis Mushayt airfield, near the Yemeni border, was enlarged and the Lightnings and Hunters operated from there, many of them flown by seconded British pilots. Also covered under the "Magic Carpet" agreement was the delivery of twenty-five BAC 167 Strikemaster Mk.80s.

The main order for forty new Lightnings was executed in 1968-69 while the helicopter force was strengthened by the addition of sixteen AB-206As and twenty-four AB-205s between 1968-70. Two C-130Es had been purchased in 1965, along with a further five during 1967/68, while two C-130Hs entered service in 1970. A total of fifty-five C-130s would eventually be operated by the RSAF, including a number of aerial tankers.

The importance of training was emphasized in 1970 by the creation of the King Faisal Air College at Riyadh, which carried out courses for both pilots and technicians, successful graduates being paid handsome

In 1985, a major arms deal was concluded with BAe. The RSAF ordered forty-eight Tornado IDS variants, the first of which were taken from RAF production allocations for immediate delivery to the RSAF. These Tornados, 701 and 704, carry the desert camouflage scheme developed specifically for the RSAF Tornados. The recent conclusion of a contract for seventy-two F-15 Strike Eagles cast doubts over further Saudi Tornado purchases. (BAe)

A Royal Saudi Air Force F-5F rolls out after landing. The F-5F is used as a conversion trainer, advanced trainer, weapons trainer and Fast FAC (Forward Air Controller). (Northrop)

salaries as an incentive to remain in service. The availability of the Lightnings, Hunters and the re-armed Sabres enabled retaliatory raids to be mounted against Yemeni strongholds before hostilities ended in 1970.

The RSAF was by now taking shape as a respectable air arm. With forty-six Lightning F.53/T.55s, the Hunters could be disposed of, while the Strikemaster force provided combined advanced training and light strike tasks. The Sabres lingered on operationally until the mid-1970s, while the T-33As served in the training role until both the Shooting Star and Sabre were replaced by Northrop F-5Bs and F5Es respectively, twenty of the F-5Bs entering service during 1972. The transport element was adequately served by the Hercules fleet while training continued both at home and in the UK, U.S. and Pakistan. The thirty Maverick-equipped F-5Es ordered in 1971 were reinforced by an additional seventy, these having both a ground attack and air combat role.

The soaring oil prices of the mid-1970s brought great wealth to Saudi Arabia which enabled it not only to upgrade its own armed forces but also those of friendly Arab states. The RSAF showed interest in 1976 in the F-15 Eagle, and some sixty aircraft were required to replace the Lightnings. In 1978, in spite of vehement Israeli protests, approval for the F-15 sale was given by the U.S., which had already given its go-ahead to the sale of F-15s to Israel and F-14s to Iran, both countries being considered as potential enemies by Saudi Arabia.

The first F-15C/Ds arrived in Dhahran in 1982, after a three year argument over whether the aircraft should be delivered with conformal fuel tanks and multiple-ejection racks which would turn them from a defensive into an offensive weapon. In the end the Saudi view prevailed, as **The BAe-RSAF deal also included the purchase of thirty Hawk Mk 65s, the first four of which were delivered in October of 1987. The aircraft are camouflaged in a three-tone Sand/Dark Green/Dark Earth wrap-around scheme and are serialed 2110 to 2139. The Hawks replaced the Strikemaster and equip Nos 21 and 37 Squadrons. (BAe)**

A pair of No 13 Squadron F-15Cs flying over the Saudi coast during 1988. Three RSAF F-15 units took an active part in Operation DESERT STORM against Iraq in 1991, a fourth squadron, No 42, being formed with an emergency delivery of twenty-four ex-USAF F-15s. One Saudi pilot, Captain A. Salah al Shamrani of No 13 Squadron, made the only non-U.S. aerial kill of the war when he downed two Iraqi Mirage F.1s during a single sortie on 24 January 1991. (MacDonnell-Douglas)

did their request for five Boeing E-3A Sentry AWACS aircraft during 1985. Included in the upgrade of the RSAF was a comprehensive C3 system as the ground component of the Saudi air defense infrastructure, and an order for a further five F-5E Tiger IIs and ten RF-5E Tigereyes.

In 1983, Saudi Arabia became interested in the Panavia Tornado both in its IDS and ADV versions. obviously for reasons of diversifying its arms sources, but mostly because of the vocal opposition of U.S. Jews each time advanced U.S. military equipment was required. Saudi Arabia was then in the geographical midst of the Iran-Iraq War, the former threatening on more than one occasion to attack Saudi Arabia for its support of Iraq. On one occasion, RSAF aircraft shot down Iranian F-4s that were engaged in anti-shipping strikes in the Gulf.

In 1985, when the Congress again refused Saudi requests for the supply of F-15E Strike Eagles, BAe clinched one of the largest defense contracts ever when the RSAF ordered forty-eight Tornado IDS variants, twenty-three Tornado ADVs, thirty BAe Hawks, two Jetstream Mk.31 navigational trainers and thirty BAe-delivered Pilatus PC-9s. This contract, known as the A1 Yamamah Program was worth some six billion

Having operated the piston-engined Provost T.53s, the Sudan Air Force followed these trainers with the purchase of twelve Jet Provost T.51 and T.52 armed jet trainers during 1962/63. Two were lost early in their careers, this aircraft (124) was lost in a crash on 13 June 1963. Serials were spread out and ranged from 124 to 195. This aircraft is armed with rockets and practice bombs on its underwing pylons. The Jet Provost could also carry gun and rocket pods. (BAC)

dollars. In order to satisfy Saudi requests for early deliveries, twenty Tornado GR.1s were diverted from the RAF production line in 1986, by which time Saudi pilots had undergone courses with the TTTE at Cottesmore and the TWCU at Honington on RAF Tornado GR.1s. Pilots destined for the ADV version took their training with the RAF's No 229 OCU at Conningsby.

The first Hawk Mk.65s were delivered in August of 1987, while the first Tornado ADVs were handed over to the RSAF in February of 1989. In the meantime, deliveries from the U.S. included five E-3As and eight KE-3A tankers in September of 1987. In Phase II of the A1 Yamamah Program, eighty-eight Westland-built Sikorsky WS-70 Black Hawks, sixty additional BAe Hawks, including a number of singleseat Mk.200s, twelve Tornado IDSs, thirty-six Tornado ADVs, twelve BAe 125s. four BAe 146 and four Jetstreams were expected to be ordered, while included in the contract was the construction of two air bases at As Sulayyi and Taiba.

The contract was later drastically revised, the extra Tornados being cancelled and partly offset by additional Hawks, while the Black Hawk order was reduced to fifty machines.

Following the end of the Iran-Iraq war in 1988, Saudi Arabia signed a non-aggression pact with Iraq. The embryo Royal Saudi Land Forces Aviation Command finally started to take shape with the acquisition of thirteen UH-60 Desert Hawks direct from Sikorsky in January of 1990 and an order for fifteen Bell 406CS Combat Scouts.

In August of 1990, Iraq invaded Kuwait, and Saudi Arabia felt threatened by Saddam Hussein's strong army and air force. The Saudi's felt they would be next on the list for invasion. Appealing for assistance, U.S., Britain, France and other nations troops and aircraft, including those from other Arab countries, were deployed to the Gulf area, mostly to bases in Saudi Arabia. The story of DESERT STORM is well known, but it is less known that RSAF Tornados and Eagles were in action. The Tornados flew in the interdiction role and the Eagles were credited with two Iraqi Mirage F.1 kills. The war also served Saudi Arabian interests, enabling it to receive an emergency military package from the U.S. in the form of priority deliveries of twenty-four ex-USAF, as well as twelve new production F-15C/Ds. A longer term arms delivery program, trimmed from twenty-one billion dollars to 6.7 billion after protests from the pro-Israeli lobby in the U.S., included seventy-two F-15S fighters, which are a version of the F-15E, twelve AH-64 Apaches, eight UH-60 Black Hawks, Patriot missiles and other military hardware.

After the destruction of a good part of the Iraqi armed forces, Saudi Arabia has emerged as the strongest power in the Gulf region, although a re-emerging Iran, might pose a challenge to Saudi Arabia,

Sudan

Silakh al Jawwiya as Sudaniye (Sudan Air Force)

Sudan gained independence from Anglo-Egyptian rule on 1 January 1956, and the following year an air arm, controlled by the Sudan Armed Forces was formed. The air arm had, as its primarily mission, internal security and policing. Its first equipment consisted of four Gomhouria Mk 2 primary trainers donated by Egypt after twelve Sudanese pilots had undergone training at the Egyptian Air Force College at Bilbeis during 1955.

With British assistance, the Sudan Air Force (SAF) was reformed as the an autonomous force. Training of the twelve pilots continued in the U.K. on Hunting Provost T.53 armed trainers, four of which had been purchased by the SAF during 1956. In November of 1957, two of the Provosts collided in mid-air, killing four of the Sudan's twelve qualified pilots.

The SAF established a Flying School at Khartoum that same year with the assistance of a RAF mission. Two replacement and three additional Provost were procured in 1958 and 1961, after a 1957 Czech offer of MiG-15 fighters was refused. A transport capability was added when

Exported to the Sudan Air Force under the designation Jet Provost T.55, the BAC 145 was, in effect, a low-powered variant of the Strikemaster light strike aircraft. Sudan purchased five which were painted in overall Light Aircraft Gray with Dayglo Red areas on the rear fuselage, nose and wingtip fuel tanks. (Author)

A single Beagle B.206S Basset was ordered by the Sudanese government and was delivered with the civil registration ST-ADA in the summer of 1969. The aircraft carried a Sudanese Air Force fin flash. (Author)

Sudan flew a number of MiG-21MF Fishbed J fighters during the late 1970s. This aircraft carries the roundel on the nose with the aircraft serial, 345, repeated on the nose and behind the wing in both Arabic and English. (USAF)

one Hunting Pembroke C.54 and two C.55s were purchased in 1959/60 and two DC-3s were obtained during 1962, crew training taking place at RAF Abingdon. Britain consolidated its Sudanese market when eight Hunting Jet Provost T.51 armed trainers were purchased in 1962/63, supplementing the piston-engined Provosts in the close support role.

Sudan is a large country with difficult land communications. Additionally, growing hostility between the Negroid minority in the south and the Arab majority in the North necessitated the modernization of the troop carrying unit. In 1965, four Fokker F.27 Troopship Mk 400Ms were purchased to join the Dakotas and Pembrokes. These were backed up by three Dornier Do 27As donated by the West German government during 1964 and eight Pilatus PC-6 Turbo-Porters purchased in 1966. The resident RAF training mission in Khartoum was influential in the sale of five BAC 145 Jet Provost T.55s to the SAF in 1969.

The Arab-Israeli war of June 1967 alienated Sudan from Britain, while the USSR was already establishing itself as Sudan's most important economic partner. In 1968, a major arms deal with the Soviets was concluded, while a 1969 army coup sent the country further towards the left. The RAF withdrew their contingent that year, promptly being replaced by a strong Soviet advisory mission together with six An-12 and six An-24 transports for the SAF. A helicopter unit was created in 1970 by the delivery of six Mi-4s and eight Mi-8s. President Nimeiri's contacts also attracted Chinese assistance and a combat element was formed with twenty Shenyang F-5 (MiG-17F) fighter-bombers with an accompanying number of FT-5 and three FT-2 (MiG-15UTI) trainers.

That same year the Shenyang F-5s were used in combat when they attacked southern villages during a sudden flare up of north-south fighting. It has been speculated that, since no Sudanese pilots had qualified on the MiGs, the pilots were probably Soviet, Chinese or Egyptian.

Another Sudanese-Soviet arms deal provided for the supply of eighteen MiG-21MFs and two MiG-21UTIs, these, together with the Chinese fighters, equipping an air defense unit. An airfield improvement and construction program, so essential in such a large country, was initiated during this time with Soviet assistance. This close connection with

the USSR came to a sudden, but not complete, halt during 1971 when an attempted coup against Nimeiri was suspected of having Soviet support. The number of Soviet advisors was reduced drastically, Sudanese communists were executed and relations between the two countries deteriorated. As a result, the SAF suffered from spares shortages and a large number of aircraft were grounded during the mid-1970s. In 1977, the remaining Soviet military personnel in Sudan were expelled and by 1978, it was estimated that only half of the MiG-21 and An-12 force was flyable.

Feeling isolated, Sudan made overtures towards the West through Egypt and Saudi Arabia, with some success. A RAF contingent arrived in Khartoum to help put the Jet Provosts and BAC 145s back into the air, while the U.S. approved the sale of six C-130H Hercules transports, although a request for F-5Es was turned down. In 1977, four DHC-5D Buffalos, ten SA.330 Pumas, twenty MBB BD 105Cs and twelve Mirage 5Ds, with an option on a further fourteen, were ordered. This relatively large number of aircraft ordered in such a short time put a strain on the Sudanese economy and the Mirage and Puma order were cancelled. A U.S. reversal of its previous decision enabled the SAF to order ten Northrop F-5Es and two F-5Fs, while China, in 1980/81, delivered twelve Shenyang F-6 (MiG-19S) fighters and a number of FT-6 trainers. The availability of the inexpensive Chinese aircraft, and Sudan's inability to secure financial backing from Saudi Arabia, again forced Sudan to cancel the F-5E/F order.

In 1981, Libyan troops involved in the Chad civil war crossed into Sudan in pursuit of retreating Chadian troops. Egypt, with whom Sudan had signed a Defense Agreement in 1977, warned Libya to refrain from invading Sudan and when the incident was repeated in 1983, Egypt issued a warning to Libya and deployed an F-4E Phantom unit to the Sudanese border. The U.S. too spoke in favor of Sudan and announced very favorable loan terms, which would enable Sudan to obtain arms to defend itself. The F-5E/F order was revived, two F-5Es and two F-5Fs reached Sudan during 1983/84. Feeling itself fully in the Western orbit, Sudan succeeded in obtaining three of the last ten Strikemasters (Mk 90s) off the BAC production line in late 1983, these joining the three

Before 1955, Syria obtained most of its arms from western sources. Since 1957, when the first of some sixty MiG-17F Fresco C fighters were delivered, Syria has been an arms client of the Soviets. This overall Natural Metal MiG-17F has the serial (39) on the nose in Black Arabic numerials. (Author)

Israeli soldiers stand guard around a captured Syrian Air Force MiG-17F Fresco C. The aircraft was camouflaged in a Sand and Brown uppersurface pattern with Light Blue undersurfaces. The MiG-17F was flown in both the interceptor and ground attack roles. (Israeli Air Force)

older but fairly similar BAC 145 Jet Provost T.55s in a COIN unit.

The transport squadron, equipped with the C-130Hs and Buffalos, was strengthened in 1984 by the acquisition of six CASA C-212 Aviocars, two of which were fitted for maritime patrol along Sudan's Red Sea coast. A Buffalo and a F.27 Friendship were donated by Oman and South Yemen respectively during 1986. The rotary wing unit still had some Mi-8s in service and these were augmented by twelve Rumanian-built IAR-330 Pumas, equivalent to the French-built SA.330J, and by eleven Agusta-Bell AB-212s in 1986.

A squadron of MiG-23BN Floggers was donated by Libya to the SAF during 1988 but only a small number, if any, remain in service. The Flogger reportedly suffered a high loss rate while in Sudanese service. That same year, the SAF received a number of F-7M Airguard fighters, a Chinese development of the MiG-21. These joined the remaining eight or nine MiG-21PFs in the inventory and were employed in both the interceptor and ground attack roles. The war with the southern rebels seemed never-ending and the SAF suffered its share of losses to SAMs, including at least three F-5Es, one Buffalo, one C130, one Shenyang F-6, one Mi-8, one An-24, three MiG-23s and one F-27M Troopship.

The resumption of relations with Libya limited operations of the southern dissidents against the central government, but another coup in July of 1989 brought to power a radical fundamentalist regime with very close relations with Iran. The SAF is reportedly using MiG-23s supplied by Iran, which had originally belonged to the Iraqi Air Force although this remains unconfirmed. The confused and highly unstable situation, particularly the north-south war, combined with a poor economic performance, has thrown Sudan into periods of famine, and only international aid efforts have prevented hundreds of thousands of deaths. Faced with such a situation, it is unlikely that the ruling regime in Khartoum will be able to convince any sensible country to extend it financial assistance for military purposes when funds can be more properly used for humanitarian needs.

Syria
Al Quwwat al Jawwiya al Arabiya As' Souriya (Syrian Arab Air Force)

Syria was a French protectorate after the First World War, finally gaining its independence after the Second World War, in April of 1946. Syria inherited from the French, and other Allied air forces that occupied the area during the Second World War, a number of useful airfields and other installations. The Syrian Air Force (SAF), however, was still in an embryonic state when the first war with Israel broke out in May of 1948.

One of the first export orders for the Aero L-29 trainer was placed by the Syrian Air Force. A total of some sixty aircraft were purchased. The aircraft were delivered in both civil and military markings. (Via Author)

Syria was another Arab country to adopt the Aero L-39 as its standard jet advanced trainer. Fifty-five L-39ZO armed trainers were delivered beginning in 1983, followed by forty-four L-39ZA variants in 1983. (Via Author)

Recognizing the importance of air power, Syria increased its efforts to build an effective air arm and the first purchases for the new air force comprised a number of Fiat G.59-2A single seaters and G.59-2B trainers from Italy, which were assigned to dual trainer and fighter roles. Seven Ju-52/3m and six C-47 transports were acquired from France, while five Harvard and ten Chipmunk trainers were purchased from the U.K.

The first real combat aircraft arrived during 1954, when a number of Gloster Meteor F.8 jet fighters were delivered, later augmented by Meteor T.7 trainers and Meteor NF.13 all-weather fighters. The total Meteor inventory was twenty-three aircraft. Syria also received some forty reconditioned Spitfire F.22 fighters.

By 1955, however, Syria had come under the influence of the Soviets and a substantial arms deal was concluded that provided for the delivery of twenty-five MiG-15s, equipping two squadrons, and six MiG-15UTIs for use as conversion trainers. Syrian pilots undertook jet training courses in Egypt, where the Syrian MiG-15s were being assembled. The Suez crisis erupted at this time and the Anglo-French attacks on Egyptian airfields destroyed all but four of the MiG-15s destined for the SAF.

Starting from scratch, Syria again turned to the USSR, which promised sixty MiG-17s, enough for five squadrons. The first of these arrived during January of 1957, by which time Syrian pilots had already undergone MiG-17 training in the Soviet Union, Poland, as well as in Syria itself under Soviet instructors.

Beset by revolutions and counter-revolutions, Syria made advances to Egypt's President Nasser during early 1958 to unite the two countries and in February of that year, the United Arab Republic (UAR) came into being. Under the new confederation, the SyAF became a component of the UAR Air Force (*Al quwwat al Jawwiya al Gomhouriya al Arabiye*). The Soviet Bloc continued to be the only source of equipment for the UARAF, but by 1963, Syria felt it was being dominated by Egypt, and an Army officers' rebellion on 26 September 1963 led to the dissolution of the UAR as far as Syria was concerned. By then the SyAF comprised two squadrons of MiG-17F interceptors and one squadron of MiG-15bis ground attack fighters. Transport was provided by eight Il-14s and a few airworthy C-47s. Trainers were mostly Eastern types; Yak-11s, Yak-18s, Chipmunks and MiG-15UTIs, while a small helicopter element was equipped with fifteen Mi-1s/Mi-4s. Maintenance of this force and training depended wholly on Soviet Bloc advisors, mostly from Poland, Czechoslovakia and the USSR.

The years leading to the 1967 Six Day War with Israel saw the SyAF expanding qualitatively with the delivery of one regiment of three squadrons of MiG-21Fs and one unit, which was still working up, with

Syria also operated a number of Mi-24 Hind D assault helicopters. These aircraft saw widespread use in the Syrian occupation of Lebanon. The aircraft carries roundels on the fuselage sides and on the underside of the main cabin. (USN)

Il-28 bombers. The number of MiG-17s was also increased considerably, and these equipped a regiment with two squadrons of MiG-17Fs and one with all-weather MiG-17PF, plus several MiG-15bis. The training element was reinforced with a small number of Aero L 29 Delfin jet trainers, while the transport fleet included one squadron with Il-14s, and a few C-47s. For army cooperation, the SyAF had a dozen Mil Mi-4 helicopters and several flights of An-2 light transports.

Tension with Israel escalated during 1966, when an Israeli Mirage III shot down a SyAF MiG-21F over Golan on 2 July, others being similarly destroyed later that year. In April of 1967, no less than six MiG-21s were shot down by Israeli Super Mystere fighters.

The Israeli surprise attack on the first day of the Six Day War, 5 June 1967, hit the Syrian airfields of Damascus, Dumeyr, Marj Riyal, Sayqal and T4. These attacks put the SyAF out of effective use, half of its strength being destroyed on the ground. Before this happened, however, the SyAF did manage to make a raid by a dozen MiG-21s and MiG-17s on the Israeli oil refinery at Haifa and on the airfield at Manahayim, for the loss of two aircraft. Besides the loss of the strategic Golan Heights, the war cost Syria the destruction of thirty of its MiG-21Fs, twenty MiG-15s/MiG-17s, two Il-28s and three Mi-4s.

Re-equipment by the Soviet Union began immediately and by mid-1968, the numerical strength of the SyAF reached numbers equal to its strength before the war. Modernization also followed, MiG-21PFs

The purchase of forty Super Frelon helicopters from France represented the first major arms contract with a western supplier in many years. The contract was financed by Saudi Arabia, which has been trying to bring the "front line" countries away from the Soviet camp by financing equipment purchases in the West. (G. Fassari)

replacing the MiG-17PFs, while Su-7BM fighter-bombers re-equipped the MiG-15bis squadrons. In 1971, MiG-19 interceptors and Mi-8 assault helicopters were added to the inventory, this quantitative increase being paralleled to a lesser extent by an improvement in pilot skill thanks to continued Soviet training.

Batteries of SA-2 and SA-3 SAMs reached Syria in large numbers during 1972 and were positioned on strategic sites. In return, Syria granted base facilities at Latakia and Tartous to the Soviet Navy which was then increasing its presence in the Mediterranean.

The SyAF was in a better situation than it had been in 1967 when war with Israel broke out again in 1973. With over 100 MiG21PFs/MFs, forty Su-7BMs and over 120 MiG-17Fs and 17PFs, the SyAF confronted the Israeli AF with greater confidence and fought strenuously over Israel's northern frontier. Pilot quality and tactics, however, again gave the edge to the Israeli Air Force which claimed no less than 150 SyAF aircraft destroyed in the air and on the ground. This, in spite of the fact that the Arabs in general acquitted themselves with honor, Syria regaining some of the territory it had lost in Golan during 1967.

The Soviet Union had again started replacing aircraft losses, even before the cease fire was declared. Again the aim was to modernize the SyAF rather than merely restore it to its previous levels. Besides 100 MiG-21MFs, twenty Su-7BMK and forty MiG-17Fs, about seventy-five third generation MiG-21SMTs, the first MiG-23BMs and Su-20 ground attack fighters had arrived in Syria by mid-1974. During this period, the SyAF also made use of air defense experts from North Korea and North Vietnam, the latter having first-hand experience during the then ongoing Vietnam War. Antonov An-12 and Il-18 transports along with Kamov Ka-25 helicopters entered service, while Soviet assistance was extended to construct three new airfields at Abu a Dubor, Sueda and Sarat while improving existing fields. This massive Soviet assistance, in conjunction with the relative political internal stability resulting from the ascent of Hafez al Assad to power during 1970, enabled the SyAF to achieve military parity with the Egyptian Air Force, then considered the leading Arab air arm.

Moreover, the financial support of Saudi Arabia was reflected in the second half of the 1970s with the purchase of Western types for the SyAF, Saudi Arabia having abandoned Egypt after the latter had made peace with Israel and had signed the Camp David accords. Forty SA.321H Super Frelon and sixty SA.342L Gazelle helicopters were purchased from France, while two Lockheed C-130H and two L-100-30 Hercules were purchased from the U.S. Six Meridionali-built CH-47C Chinooks, twenty-four Agusta-Bell AB-212ASWs and Agusta-built SH-3D Sea Kings were purchased from Italy during 1980.

The delivery of Mach 3 MiG-25R reconnaissance fighters to the SyAF during 1979 confirmed earlier reports of a V-VS squadron of this type having been based in Syria for some time. The USSR remained the main

Eight Aermacchi MB-326Bs were delivered to the Tunisian Air Force during 1965 to establish an advanced flying school. The aircraft were later marked with an FA code on the nose in Black. (Aermacchi)

source of SyAF equipment and a quantity of MiG-21bis fighters (bringing the total for the MiG-21 to some 250) and forty of the new Mil Mi-24 assault helicopters were procured in 1980, while attempts to purchase the Italian Agusta A-109 Hitundo attack helicopter failed. By now Syrian defense needs had to take into account not only Israel but also Iraq, the Syrian and Iraqi regimes having come to a mutual dislike (in this case the regimes being in fact the two presidents, Assad and Hussein). In fact, Syria fully supported Iran during the Iran/Iraq war.

It was Israel, however, that Syria had to confront again in 1982. Syria had invaded Lebanon in support of the PLO in May of 1976, its army aided by Su-7s and MiG-21s. Israel viewed this invasion with suspicion and clashes between the SyAF and the IDF/AF over the Beka'a Valley between 1978 and 1981 resulted in two dozen Syrian aircraft being lost, including MiG-21s, MiG-23s and MiG-25s. The IDF/AF had, by then, re-equipped with F-15s and F-16s. As terrorist attacks by the PLO increased and tension mounted, Israel invaded Lebanon on 4 June 1982. Its air force, using Shrike, Standard and Maverick anti-radar missiles, soon disposed of the Syrian SAMs, while large scale dogfights took place between F-15s, F-16s, F-4s and Kfirs on one side against MiG-23s, MiG-21s and Su-7s on the other. Israeli claims totaled eighty-four aircraft (fifty-four MiG-23s/21s, two MiG-25Rs, three helicopters and twenty-five others) for thirteen admitted losses, but the Syrian claims vary widely from these figures. Although a cease fire was declared on 11 June, fighting continued, involving also RAF, French Navy and USN aircraft, which were protecting the Multi-National Force in Lebanon.

Once again Israeli supremacy in air combat had been proved, but this time modern electronic technology had won the war. The Israelis possessed the best fighters available anywhere, the F-15 and F-16, the best anti-radar missiles, and had the advantage of four E-2C Hawkeye AEW aircraft which played a crucial role in controlling combat and in jamming Syrian aircraft communications with their ground controllers. Moreover, the MiG-25Rs of the SyAF proved to be vulnerable against a Sparrow-equipped F-15. The Soviet-supplied SA-5, SA-6, SA-7, SA-8

and SA-9 SAMs were knocked out with relative ease by U.S.-built anti-radar missiles carried by Israeli fighters.

A one-for-one loss replacement was made by the Soviets so that by 1983, the SyAF could count on a force of 470 combat aircraft composed of twelve MiG-25/25Rs, ninety MiG-23 Flogger-Es/Fs, 200 MiG-21PF/MF/SMT/bis, sixty Su-7MK Fitter As, sixty Su-22 Fitter Fs and fifty MiG-17Fs, besides transports, training and helicopter types. Clearly, however, more modern types would be necessary to counter Israel's superior types and approaches were made to obtain the USSR's newest equipment such as MiG-29 Fulcrums and MiG-31 Foxhounds.

The Beka'a Valley lessons also meant the provision, in 1986, of MiG-25 Foxbat D ELINT aircraft and specially-fitted An-26 radio-relay aircraft. During July of 1987, the first of forty MiG-29s began to arrive in Syria, the aircraft having simpler avionics than those in V-VS service. Syrian pilots were sent to the USSR to undertake conversion training on the type. Although passing through a difficult economic period, Syria also requested numbers of the formidable Su-24 Fencer deep penetration fighter, of which twenty of the Su-24MK version were delivered in late 1989.

The invasion of Kuwait by Syria's arch enemy Iraq gave Syria the opportunity to effect an alignment with the West. It joined the anti-Saddam Hussein coalition which defeated Iraq and freed Kuwait. Additionally, Syria has participated in the on-going peace talks with Israel on a Middle East settlement. In order to reach a successful conclusion of peace terms, Syria is insisting on the return of all territory in the Golan Heights lost during the 1967 Six Day War.

Now that Syria's main arms supplier, the USSR, no longer exists as such, it is to be seen where Syria will go to effect an upgrading of its air force. The new Russia would be willing to sell arms to improve its own economy, and a further forty-eight MiG-29s and twenty-four Su-24 Fencers are under negotiation. A successful conclusion of the ongoing peace talks could also open the door for the supply of western equipment.

Tunisia

Force Aerienne de la Republique de Tunisie, Al Quwwat al Jawwiya al Djoumhouria at' Tunisiya (Air Force of the Republic of Tunisia)

Tunisia occupies a strategic position at the narrowest part of the central Mediterranean and France moved into the territory during 1881 and established a naval base at Bizerte. France remained dominate in Tunisian affairs until, after six years of internal trouble, France granted

The first SAAB 91D Safir delivered to the Tunisian Air Force carried a large Black "1" on the fin and the serial Y31001. The aircraft was overall Blue-Gray with a Black anti-glare panel. The Safirs were based at El Aouina and remained in service for some fifteen years. (Author)

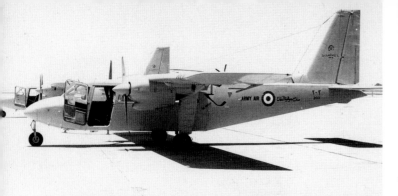

This Hawker Hunter F.76A of the Abu Dhabi Army Air Force was camouflaged in a pattern of Dark Earth and Light Earth uppersurfaces over Azure Blue undersurfaces with a thin Red demarcation line running the length of the fuselage. (Author)

Abu Dhabi Army Air Force aircraft carried the legend Army Air and their serial on the fuselage side in both English and Arabic. Roundels were carried in six positions. Later the legend was changed from Army Air to Air Force. (Author)

The first of three BN-2A Islanders for the Abu Dhabi Army Air Wing arrived during 1968. Delivered in an overall Sand camouflage scheme, the Islanders were serialed 201-203. Aircraft 202 was delivered on 19 March 1969 and remained in service until sold to the Somali Air Force in 1983. (Via Author)

the country independence in 1956, retaining control of Bizerte naval base. One year later a republican regime toppled the local ruler in a bloodless coup.

In 1960, the government decided to form an air arm and in September nine SAAB 91D Safir trainers were purchased from Sweden for the flying school of the new *Force Aerienne de la Republique de Tunisie* (FAeRT) set up at El Aouina (Tunis-Cartage) with the assistance of the Swedish Air Force. The Swedes also accepted Moroccans for training in Sweden. Six other Safirs were procured in 1961, these and the secondment of Swedish instructors enabling further training to be given locally.

Relations with France were improved after the French relinquished control of Bizerte and an assistance agreement was concluded during 1962 which provided for a resident French military aviation mission and the supply of two SA.3130 Alouette IIs, twelve ex-French Army T-6G Texan armed trainers and three Dassault MD-315 Flamant light transports which also doubled as multi-engined trainers. France later also donated four additional Alouette IIs and four SA.316B Alouette IIIs, these forming a rotary wing communications and army liaison squadron. The air arm entered the jet age in 1965 when eight Aermacchi MB-326Bs were ordered from Italy. Advanced training on the MB-326s was undertaken in Tunisia with the help of Italian instructors.

Tunisian foreign policy was generally pro-West, the country taking an independent stand from other Arab countries even in regards to Israel. In 1969, the U.S. donated twelve ex-Japanese Air Force F-86F Sabres, these forming the first FAeRT interceptor unit. These worn-out fighters served as stop gap measure until a consignment of seven armed and uprated MB-326KTs and four two-seat MB-326LTs were delivered during 1977, the Sabres being relegated to an arms training role.

The training Safirs were replaced during 1975 by twelve SIAI SF-260WR Warrior light armed trainers, followed by nine unarmed SF-260CTs during 1978. These aircraft were purchased with Italian government credits, which also enabled the procurement of eighteen AB-205A helicopters and four SIAI S-208 light aircraft in 1979, these relieving the Flamants in the liaison and troop transport role.

Growing hostility between moderate Tunisia and its more militant Libyan neighbor came to a head in February of 1980 when an attempted uprising in central Tunisia was blamed on Libya. A more effective deterrent was clearly required if the FAeRT was to defend Tunisian airspace and in 1981 a $300 million deal was made with Northrop for the supply of six F-5Es and six F-5Fs. Six Bell 205A-1s, six Aerospatiale SA.350B Ecureils and two C-130H Hercules were also contracted for during 1982.

Limited expansion of the FAeRT has been made since then, except for the purchase of seven ex-USAF F-5Es during 1989. During 1992, consideration was given to purchasing twelve Aero L-59 Albatros trainers from Czechoslovakia as replacements for the aging MB-326s and an agreement was concluded during early 1994.

United Arab Emirates
United Arab Emirates Air Force

When Britain was planning to withdraw from the Persian Gulf, it encouraged the group of sheikdoms and emirates which it had protected, known as the Trucial States, to form a confederation known as the United Arab Emirates. All the former Trucial States, except Qatar and Bahrain, assented to the Union: Abu Dhabi, Ajman, Dubai, Fujaira, Ras al-Khaimah, Sharjah and Umm al-Qaiwan. The loose federation came into being, politically, in December of 1971. Prior to this, Abu Dhabi, the wealthiest of the group, had already formed its own air arm and it was around this force that the UAE/AF was eventually established.

The Abu Dhabi Army Air Wing (ADAAW) was formed in 1968 with British assistance as a communications element with two AB-206Bs and three BN.2A Islanders, a fourth Islander and two other AB-206As being added later. Increasing oil income permitted the formation of a combat

Helicopters in the Abu Dhabi Air Force were serialed in the 100 range. This was the third Puma helicopter (serial 111) delivered, it was followed by seven additional Pumas. During 1983, a second contract was awarded by Abu Dhabi for ten Super Pumas. (Author)

The DHC-4 Carlbou's short take-off capability was well suited to Abu Dhabi's early desert strips. Four aircraft were purchased during 1969/1970, painted in a Sand and Brown over Light Blue camouglage scheme. The aircraft were serialed 301-304, a fifth aircraft, number 305, was delivered in June of 1971. (M. Pace)

Serialed 101, this SA.319B Alouette III was the first of five delivered to the ADAF during 1972. They were followed by another batch of five during 1975. (G. J. Kamp)

unit and in March of 1970, ten refurbished Hawker Hunter F.76s and two Hunter T.77 trainers were delivered, flown by seconded RAF pilots and maintained under contract with a British firm. Four DHC Caribous were purchased in 1969/71 for transport duties, other purchases included five SA.330C Pumas and five SA.319B Alouette IIIs in 1972, the latter augmenting the AB-206s.

An update of the combat element soon became necessary and in 1972 fourteen Mirage 5ADs/5DADs were ordered from France, the air arm changing its name to Abu Dhabi Air Force (ADAF) that same year. Pakistani Air Force personnel were hired on an indefinite secondment to fly the Mirages which were operated from Abu Dhabi International Airport. The UAE having by then been formed, the Hunters were transferred to the ex-RAF base at Sharjah.

The Dubai Police Air Wing had been formed in 1971 with a Cessna 185 and two Bell 206B Jet Rangers, a further AB-206 and two Bell 205As being soon added. In 1974, three Aermacchi MB-326KDs and one MB-326LD were ordered to form a combat element, the change of duties also resulting in renaming the force from Dubai Police Air Wing to Dubai Defense Force Air Wing.

Painted in a complex but attractive camouflage, this Aermacchi MB-326LD at Venegono, Italy, prior to delivery carries the insignia of the UAE/AF instead of the insignia of the Dubai Air Force. From the fourth aircraft onwards, the UAE/AF's insignia was applied to the MB-326s at the factory, while the first three were repainted at their next overhaul period. (G. Fassari)

The Mirage 5AD represented the ADAF's first new combat aircraft and was, without doubt, the major contribution to the new United Arab Emirates Air Force on its formation. Mirage 5 deliveries started in 1978 and a total of thirty-two were purchased. Mirage 5AD and 5EAD fighters carried serials in the 400 and 500 range respectively. (G. J. Kamp)

Although one of the aims of the UAE air arms was standardization of equipment, both Abu Dhabi and Dubai apparently retained a certain degree of independence in arms procurement. The former became predominantly a French arms buyer, while Dubai purchased all its aircraft from Italy, including four additional MB-326s, an Aeritalia G.222 transport and a SIAI SF-260WD trainer.

Abu Dhabi also made a repeat order for three Mirage 5RAD reconnaissance fighters and a Mirage 5DAD trainer while later in 1976, no less than fourteen Mirage 5EADs, three 5RADs and one 5DAD were purchased to equip a second unit deployed to Sharjah.

The formal integration of the military components of the seven states was finalized as planned in May of 1976, after which all aircraft were to carry the same Union national insignia, although many aircraft had to wait until they were due for repainting to effect the markings change.

Both Abu Dhabi and Dubai ordered BAe Hawks during 1983, the former receiving sixteen Mk 63s. All were painted in a Dark Earth/Light Stone uppersurface camouflage pattern with Light Blue undersurfaces and carry UAE/AF national insignia. Abu Dhabi Hawks are serialed 1001 to 1016. In 1991 plans were made to upgrade the aircraft to Mk.63A standards (Hawk Mk 102). Eighteen Hawk Mk 102s were also ordered in 1989. (J. Visanich

A line-up of Hawk Mk 63s of the Abu Dhabi element of the UAE/AF. This batch, serialed 1011 to 1013, was transiting through Luqa, Malta on 29 March 1985 on their delivery flight to Abu Dhabi. They are now based at Al Dhafra with the Flying Training School. (J. Visanich)

An Abu Dhabi Hawk Mk 63 (1016) on touch down at Luqa, Malta during its delivery flight. It was accompanied by two other Hawks (1014 and 1015) and reached Abu Dhabi via Luxor, Egypt. (J. Visanich)

Again, arms procurement sources varied, and Abu Dhabi ordered two C-l30H Hercules transports, two Shorts Skyvan 3Ms and four DHC-5D Buffalos for transport duties.

An infrastructural program for Abu Dhabi in the late 1970s included the construction of new military air bases at Taif and Al Harma. Training, too, was given importance and in 1981 an order for fourteen Pilatus PC-7s, later increased to twenty-four, was placed with Switzerland. Dubai ordered six SIAI SF-260TPs in 1983.

The need for an aircraft capable of replacing the Hunter for close-support and advanced training in the ADAF was fulfilled when sixteen BAe Hawk Mk 63s were ordered. Dubai, which was already operating the MB-326, accepted an offer for four of the improved MB-339As but pressure from Abu Dhabi, to avoid multiplicity of equipment resulted in a Dubai placeing an order for eight Hawk Mk 61s as well!

Favorable petroleum prices made it possible for Abu Dhabi to finalize a contract in 1983 for the delivery of eighteen Mirage 2000s, with an option for a further eighteen being taken up a year later, in an oil-for-arms deal. A dispute as to what U.S. equipment had been specified in the contract delayed deliveries to November of 1989, when the first six aircraft were delivered. Quantities varied slightly from the original contract and comprised twenty-two Mirage 2000EAD interceptors, eight Mirage 2000RAD reconnaissance fighters and six Mirage 2000DAD trainers. One of the latter crashed in January of 1990 prior to delivery, while the last of the thirty-five aircraft on order was handed over in October of 1991. Eighteen enhanced laser-nosed BAe Hawk Mk 102s were delivered in 1993, while the fifteen surviving Hawk Mk 63s have been upgraded to a hybrid variant, the Mk 63/100 version, known as Mk 63C. The first of twenty AH-64A Apaches was delivered in late 1993 to equip an anti-armor helicopter force.

A third member of the UAE, Sharjah, established an air arm in December of 1984 at Murgab. Named the Amiri Guard Air Wing, the force was formed with one Bell 206B, a Shorts Skyvan 3M, with a Shorts 330UTT being added in 1986. The air wing soon moved to

This DHC-2 Beaver (serial 302) was one of three which formed the first equipment of the short-lived South Arabian Air Force. The unusual South Arabian roundel was soon replaced by a triangular marking, used by the South Yemen Air Force after independence. (Via Author)

Two UAE/AF Mirage 2000EADs (one 741) formate with a Mirage 2000DAD trainer (705) over France. The trainer carries an air-superiority two tone Gray camouflage, while the single seat fighters carry a desert tactical camouflage. None of the aircraft carry fuselage roundels, only fin flashes and unit badges on the nose. (AMD-BA)

Shariah International Airport, having procured a further two Jet Rangers and two MBB-Kawasaki BK-117 helicopters. Again, the Sharjah air arm seems to operate independently of the UAE/AF.

Although rather disjointed, with the two main contributors pursuing their own procurement policies, the UAE/AF's ultimate aim is total integration. A step in this direction was made in 1986 when the UAE/AF was re-organized into two commands: the Western Command with responsibility of Al Dhafra air base (Il Shaheen unit with Mirage 5s, Al Ghazelle unit with Gazelles, and the FTS with PC-7s and Hawks), Bateen air base (Transport Wing) and Sharjah airport (I Shaheen unit with Mirage 5s) and the Central Command, controlling Mindhat air base (III Shaheen unit with Hawks, Flying Training Academy with SF-260s, MB-339s and MB-326s, and a Transport Squadron). There have also been a substantial number of aircraft carrying civil registrations which are used by the several sheiks and their officials on government business. These include Boeing 707s, 720s, 727s, 737s and 747s, a VC10, Gulfstream 1159s, Falcon 20s and Falcon 900s.

The UAE/AF is, at present, seeking additional advanced fighter aircraft, the main contenders being the Mirage 2000-5, F-15E Strike Eagle, F-18 Hornet, MiG-29 Fulcrum and Su-27 Flanker.

Yemen
Al Quwwat al Jawwiya al Yemeniya (Yemeni Air Force)

The former Yemen Arab Republic (North Yemen) and the Democratic People's Republic of the Yemen (South Yemen) were united formally in May of 1990 to form one nation. Often at odds with each other in the past, even going to war in 1979, the two countries had long been making attempts at unification. Basic ideological differences were thought to have been successfully overcome, and the discovery of further oil and gas reserves gave a sense of optimism to the Yemenis who, having sided with Iraq during the invasion of Kuwait in 1990, have paid dearly for their decision.

Four years after unification, however, a civil war between north and south broke out on 4 May 1994, with heavy fighting and air strikes being mounted against each other's regions. The northerners took the upper hand and by early June had surrounded Aden, which southern secessionists had proclaimed their capital, after repudiating the union between the traditionalist north and the former Marxist south. Aden fell to the northern troops on 7 July, ending the southerners' hopes of re-establishing an independent South Yemen.

Since for most of the period under review the two Yemens were still separate nations, each with its own policies and equipment, their air forces will be dealt with as individual organizations.

Yemen Arab Republic (North Yemen)

Al Quwwat al Jawwiya al Jamhuroiya al Arabiyaal Yemeniya (Yemen Arab Republic Air Force)

Prior to the Yemeni-Egyptian agreement of 1956 by which an Egyptian military mission started to train Yemen's armed forces, what military aircraft were available were regarded as the Imam's private air fleet rather than a national air force. These aircraft included a couple of T-6 Texans and Aero Commanders, three Cessna AT-17 Bobcats, three C-47s and a Noorduyn Norseman operated by Swedish and, later, U.S. personnel under contract.

After 1956, Yemen entered Egypt's orbit and a Czech military mission, together with twelve Ilyushin Il-10 ground-attack aircraft and four Avia C-11 (Yak-11) trainers arrived the following year to equip the newly-formed Yemen Arab Republic Air Force (YARAF).

Soviet and eastern Bloc crews soon took over from U.S. personnel and in 1958, Yemen became part of the United Arab Republic along with Egypt and Syria. Modernization of desert strips and the construction of new airfields, particularly near the border with the British-held Aden Protectorate (later to become South Yemen), were carried out by Soviets. The Yemeni Imam had long claimed sovereignty over Aden and brief fighting was reported in 1958 when Yemeni troops invaded the Protectorate until they were driven out and order restored.

The Soviets strengthened the YARAF with both aircraft and crews. The number of Il-10s was increased to thirty-six, Mi-4 helicopters were delivered for army cooperation, these being flown by Soviet crews, and thirty Yak-11s were donated for training purposes. On the death of the Imam in September of 1962, army officers carried out a coup which led to civil war between the Republicans, led by the coup leader and supported by Egypt, and the Royalists aided by Saudi Arabia. The YARAF took little part in the fighting that ensued, although Egyptian Air Force MiG17s, MiG-15s and Il-28s roamed and attacked royalist strongholds at will. In fact, support for the air force was abandoned and no new equipment added. The withdrawal of Egyptian and Saudi forces in 1967 and the subsequent defeat of the royalists encouraged the re-establishment of the YARAF in 1970. The Soviets supplied one squadron of MiG-17 fighter-bombers, one of Il-28 light bombers, four MiG-15UTI trainers, additional Mi-4s and a unit of Il-14 transports, plus an advisory and training mission. In return, the Soviets gained access to base facilities at San'a, Hodeida and Janad, but in spite of these close relations, North Yemen was not drawn completely into the Soviet sphere of influence, a nonaligned policy being adopted and contacts re-established with the West and with Saudi Arabia. Two AB-204Bs and two AB-205s were purchased from Italy and two Alouette IIIs arrived from France while two Short Skyvan 3Ms were ordered from Britain in 1974/75.

Meanwhile, the neighboring Aden Protectorate, on gaining independence, became practically a Soviet satellite and adopted the name Democratic People's Republic of Yemen (South Yemen). Armed with

The YARAF operates at least twelve Mi-8 Hip assault helicopters augmented by a number of western types such as the AB-204 and AB-205. The aircraft were based at Hodelda.

MiG-17s and MiG-21s and assisted by a Cuban military delegation, South Yemen posed a threat to North Yemen which in 1975, turned to the U.S. for the supply of Northrop F-5 fighters. It was not until 1978 that the U.S. gave its approval for Saudi Arabia to transfer four F-5Bs to the YARAF and the purchase, with Saudi funds, of twelve F-5E Tiger IIs and two C-130H Hercules from the U.S. in 1979.

In February of that year, war broke out between the two Yemens after attempts at unification failed. South Yemen's troops invaded North Yemen but Saudi and Syrian mediation brought about a cease fire in March. Although border skirmishes continued well into August, the two Yemens renewed unification talks, the immediate results of which were fresh overtures to North Yemen from the Soviets who resumed arms deliveries in late 1979/early 1980 including ten MiG-21s, twenty Su-22s, three An-24s and three An-26s accompanied by advisors and technicians who helped to return a number of MiG-15s, MiG-17s and Il-28s to flyable condition after having been grounded for some years at Taiz and Hodeida.

By 1983, the air defense command comprised twenty-five MiG-21MFs at Hodelda and twelve Taiwanese-flown F-5Es at San'a, while the Cuban-flown Su-22s formed the ground-attack force. Transports included C-130s, An-24s, An-26s and several Dakotas. From 1984 to 1986, three Fokker F.27 Friendships were also operated as part of the transport unit. The helicopter fleet comprised twelve Mi-8s augmented by several Western types.

Little progress towards modernization of the YARAF took place during the 1980s while unification talks, held at irregular intervals, came to fruition in May of 1990, with the merging of the two countries. Sympathy with Iraq prevailed during the Iraqi invasion of Kuwait the following August and the united Yemen was even reported to have delivered arms to Iraq. Although Yemen later condemned the invasion, Saudi Arabia cut its subsidies and expelled almost a million Yemeni workers. Until the present oil and gas drilling starts to yield a steady income, there is little hope that the YARAF will be able to purchase modern aircraft.

The new South Yemen national markings were carried by four BAC Strikemaster Mk 81s (serials 501-504) delivered in August of 1969. The aircraft were camouflaged in an uppersurface pattern of Dark Earth/Dark Green with Light Aircraft Gray undersurfaces. (Author)

A BAC Strikemaster Mk 81 on final approach for landing. The Strikemasters did not have long service careers in South Yemen, being sold to Singapore during 1975/76, after being replaced by Soviet equipment. (Author)

Peoples Democratic Republic of Yemen (South Yemen)

Al Quwwat al Jawwiya al Jumhuriya al Yemen al Dimuqratiya al Sha'abiya (Air Force of the People's Democratic Republic of Yemen)

The Colony of Aden had been in British hands since 1839 and over the years the Protectorate came to comprise a large area west and northeast of Aden proper. In 1959, the Federation of South Arabia was formed, with British approval, within the boundaries of the eastern Protectorate. The western part joined the Federation in 1963, so when the British left in 1967, the enlarged Federation became an independent nation.

A South Arabian Air Force had been established within a defense set-up at Khormaksar (Aden) in mid-1967 by the British to deter a possible invasion by North Yemen, which claimed the territory. The first aircraft being three DHC Beavers, soon followed by three others, three C-47s and six Westland Sioux (Bell 47G-3s) donated by Britain. For policing duties, eight armed Jet Provost T.52s (converted from ex-RAF T.4s) were delivered. On Britain's departure, however, a leftist front deposed the leaders and proclaimed the South Yemen People's Republic, with a strong leaning towards the USSR, the air force becoming known as the Air Force of the South Yemen People's Republic (AFSYPR). The promised donation by Britain of a number of Hawker Hunters was withheld, but the AFSYPR still had on order four BAC Strikemaster Mk 81s which, in the event, were delivered in August of 1969.

The AFSYPR refused British technical assistance and in 1969 a large Soviet military advisory and training mission arrived, soon followed by a squadron of MiG-21Fs, which were operated by Soviet pilots from Khormaksar. A unit of MiG-17Fs was shipped late in the year, these being flown by South Yemenis trained in the USSR. By 1972, South Yemenis were able to fly the MiG-21s and by that time a Cuban mission had partly replaced the Soviets at Khormaksar and other airfields. Progressive phasing out of British equipment was effected, some of the Jet Provosts and the four Strikemasters being sold to Singapore in 1975/76. Border clashes along the undefined frontiers with Saudi Arabia, North Yemen and Oman were frequent, particularly with Oman, South Yemen having given assistance and sanctuary to the Maoist Dhofari guerrillas who operated against the Omani government. In March of 1973, MiG-17Fs of the Peoples Democratic Republic of Yemen (AFPDRY) supported an attack on Saudi border positions, the MiGs allegedly being flown by Cuban pilots.

By 1978, Soviet Navy Il-38 maritime reconnaissance aircraft were being deployed to the Indian Ocean flying from Mukalla on long range patrols of the Indian Ocean, regularly overflying ships of western navies. South Yemen projected Soviet policy onto the Horn of Africa and AFPDRY pilots are believed to have flown MiG fighters in Ethiopia against Eritrean rebels. In return, the Soviets supplied arms and by 1979 had supplied some fifty MiG-21s, thirty Su-22s and forty MiG-17s. Transport deliveries included four An-24s and four Il-14s. Six to seven Il-28 bombers were also on hand as were eight Mi-8 and some Mi-4 helicopters. Most Western equipment, except for three/four C-47s were either disposed of or placed in long term storage. MiG-15UTI trainers were provided for the training of local pilots by the Cuban and Soviet missions.

A short war between North and South Yemen broke out in February of 1979 after attempts at unification failed, and PDRY forces invaded North Yemen, withdrawing the following month, after mediation by Syria and Saudi Arabia. After this episode, which was accompanied in the following months by low-scale border skirmishes, the two Yemens started a series of talks on unification.

Economic difficulties during the 1980s precluded the desired expansion of the AFPDRY and although more modern variants of the MiG-21 Fishbed (MiG-21MF and PF), twenty-five MiG-23BMs and fifteen Mi-24 Hind helicopter gunships were added to the inventory in 1986, no other significant deliveries were recorded. South Yemen's economic plight was severe and in the early 1980s a change in leadership brought about a re-approachement with the pro-West Gulf states. In 1986, however, a coup assisted by the USSR, put a staunchly Communist leadership back in power, Soviet aircraft based in the country even taking part in the short battles that ensued. That same year, the deployment of Soviet Il-38s, which had ceased in the early 1980s, resumed, followed by V-VS MiG-25R reconnaissance fighter operations. Foreign military missions, by 1988, totaled some 40,000 Soviets, Cubans, North Koreans and East Germans, while use of South Yemeni territory by the Soviets included the naval and air facilities at Perim Island, and the anchorage at Socotra. Considering the small number of training aircraft in the AFPDRY inventory, it is almost certain that most training was carried out overseas, probably in Eastern Europe.

Unification brought a short respite of peace, but the May/July 1994 civil war with northern Yemen again threw the country into difficulties. Combat aircraft stationed in southern Yemen took an active part in the civil war but, like their northern counterparts, the air force high command lacked cohesive plans for air defense or for effective ground support. The north army's greater strength prevailed over the south's superiority in the air and gained it the upper hand, the south's hopes of dissolution from the 1990 union coming to an end when Aden fell on 7 July 1994.

During the fighting, it was reported that the south had obtained a number of MiG-29s flown by Eastern European and Syrian pilots recruited by Kuwait and Saudi Arabia on behalf of the south. In addition, sixteen MiG-21s and twelve Su-22 Fitters were also reportedly supplied to the southern forces. As the south was falling, a number of aircraft were reportedly flown to neighboring countries and the northern government has made a formal request to the Arab League for return of all such aircraft. The MiG-29s and MiG-21s did see action during their brief service with the south, reportedly raiding the Marib oil field on 30 June 1994.

This An-24 Coke turboprop transport of the AFPDRY was intercepted over the Red Sea by U.S. Navy fighters on 19 March 1979. It carries the new roundel insignia that replaced the early triangle marking carried on the Provost and Strikemaster aircraft. The fin flash has been noted as a rudder marking (similar to the Cuban Air Force rudder stripes) on MiG-21MF Fishbed J fighters intercepted over the Red Sea by U.S. Navy aircraft. (USN via Nicholas J. Waters III)